PE
1128
A2
F474
2011

Treatment of Error in Second Language Student Writing

Second Edition

Dana R. Ferris

University of California, Davis

D1257300

The Michigan Series on Teaching Multilingual Writers

Series Editors: Diane Belcher and Jun Liu

Ann Arbor
The University of Michigan Press

BERGEN COMMUNITY COLLEGE LIBRARY

 **The Michigan Series on Teaching Multilingual Writers**

Series Editors
Diane Belcher (Georgia State University) and
Jun Liu (Georgia State University)

Available titles in the series

Copyright © by the University of Michigan 2011
All rights reserved
Published in the United States of America
The University of Michigan Press
Manufactured in the United States of America

♾ Printed on acid-free paper

ISBN-13: 978-0-472-03476-5

2014   2013   2012   2011   4   3   2   1

No part of this publication may be reproduced, stored
in a retrieval system, or transmitted in any form or
by any means, electronic, mechanical, or otherwise,
without the written permission of the publisher.

Library of Congress Cataloging-in-Publication Data

Ferris, Dana.
    Treatment of error in second language student writing / Dana R.
Ferris. — 2nd ed.
        p. cm.
    Includes bibliographical references and index.
    ISBN 978-0-472-03476-5 (pbk. : alk. paper)
    1. English language—Study and teaching—Foreign speakers. 2. English
language—Rhetoric—Study and teaching. 3. Report writing—Study and teaching. 4. English language—Errors of usage. 5. Second language acquisition.
I. Title.
    PE1128.A2F474 2011
    808'.0428071--dc23   2011023791

To the scholars and teachers out there who are trying hard to do the right thing on a sticky issue. You inspire me.

Series Foreword

Approximately a decade and a dozen books ago, our series was launched with the publication of Dana Ferris's *Treatment of Error in Second Language Student Writing*. It is difficult to imagine a more auspicious start for a series. As soon as it appeared in print, *Treatment of Error* found an eager and extensive audience and, since then, has continued to appeal to a wide readership. Those who have read the first edition, perhaps repeatedly as have many of us who view it as a trusted guide to addressing multilingual writers' language use issues and to teaching others how to do so, should be more than pleased to see Ferris's updated and expanded second edition, enhanced by insights from recent developments in areas such as second language acquisition and corpus linguistics. Readers for whom the second edition is their first experience with this book—whether novice or seasoned teachers, specializing in the teaching and learning of language, or just interested in helping language learners produce more reader-friendly texts—will likely find in this highly accessible, practitioner-oriented resource the type of guidance that they are seeking and are unlikely to find elsewhere.

No specific prior training is needed to benefit from the research- and theory-informed journey Ferris takes us on through the challenging terrain of responding to error. Far from downplaying the challenge, Ferris heightens our appreciation of the complexity of the undertaking—helping learners' take control of the syntactic, morphological, and lexical dimensions of their texts—while at the same providing us with a highly persuasive rationale for accepting this responsibility and an impressive toolkit of approaches for facilitating our students' progress. The goal of this book is not, as a facile interpretation of the title *Treatment of Error* might lead one to believe, simply to make us more efficient and effective correctors of our students' grammar. The goal is instead to enable us to better scaffold our students' growing independence as language analysts and self-editors, and ultimately as producers of second language texts that speak for them and to readers in the ways that they, as authors, want them to. Ferris's expertise in this area—responding to the linguistic needs of multilingual writers—and her understanding of the needs of those who teach them make the goal of second language learner (and writer) autonomy seem eminently achievable.

Diane Belcher
Georgia State University

Jun Liu
Georgia State University

Preface

My own interest in the treatment of error in second language (L2) student writing began, literally, in various women's restrooms on several university campuses in the latter half of the 1980s. This was where I and other ESL teachers would talk about a dilemma that we all struggled with. We had been trained to be "process approach" writing teachers (following seminal works such as Zamel, 1982, and Krashen, 1984)— encouraging multiple-drafting, revision, collaboration, and an emphasis on ideas, with attention to language issues (grammar, vocabulary, spelling, punctuation, and other mechanics) being intentionally postponed to the very end of the composing process. What this often meant, in practice, was that grammar and editing issues were almost never addressed by teachers or their students in the ESL writing classroom. And yet, we found, the students' language problems were not magically disappearing as the sure result of a more enlightened process and view of writing. Worse, L2 writers themselves, painfully aware of their own linguistic deficits and the need for teacher intervention, were disappointed with instructional policies such as, "I will not correct your journal entries, your freewrites, or your early essay drafts. You should be focusing on expressing your ideas and building fluency and not worrying about grammar until 'later.'"

This simultaneous awareness of persistent written error and of student frustration led to these whispered restroom discussions:

"I'm teaching grammar in my writing class."

"I am, too. I *have* to. They *need* it!"

To those of us trained in process philosophies and techniques, error correction, grammar instruction, and editing strategy training felt like the "dirty little secret" of our writing classes. We were ashamed because we felt we should "know better" and that we and our students should have "moved beyond" these issues. Still, our sense of what students needed overrode these considerations, and the treatment of error continued, albeit somewhat underground.

My own need to understand what might help my university ESL writers to improve the linguistic accuracy of their texts has led me over the past 15 years to pursue a variety of classroom research projects and to develop teaching materials for ESL writing classes and for teacher preparation courses. This book pulls together the results of these explorations in what I hope is a coherent and holistic approach to the treatment of error in L2 writing classes.

I would be remiss if I did not acknowledge the contributions of others to my own thinking on this topic. First and foremost, I must thank the hundreds of ESL writers and M.A. TESOL graduate students in classes at California State University, Sacramento, from 1990 to the present, who have served as willing participants in my research efforts and as test pilots for my teaching materials. I am also grateful to the many ESL teachers in the program at CSUS who generously cooperated in data collection efforts over the years and utilized my materials. In particular, I want to thank Sarah Chaney, Shelagh Nugent, Gabriella Nuttall, Barrie Roberts, and Stuart Schulz, all of whom taught in the Learning Skills Center at CSUS and allowed me and others to collect data in their classrooms; thanks also go to Professors Robby Ching and Sue McKee of the Learning Skills Center. My other colleagues in the M.A. TESOL Program in the English Department at CSUS were instrumental in shaping my thinking about grammar issues and especially about teacher preparation options. I am also grateful to CSUS for providing me with various grants of release time and funding over the years that have enabled me to carry out many of these projects and to the English Department (especially the former and current chairs, Ted Hornback and Mark Hennelly) for allowing me to accept these grants.

I must also acknowledge my former graduate students, now professional colleagues, who worked with me on research projects over the years: Sarah Chaney, Rich Harroun, Hiliry Harvey, Tina Jordan, Keiko Komura, Gabriella Nuttall, Susan Pezone, Christiana Rennie, Barrie Roberts, Cathy Tade, and Sharee Tinti. I am further indebted to many other colleagues in the field who have read my manuscripts and discussed grammar and editing issues with me over the years. I am particularly grateful for the support of series editors Diane Belcher and Jun Liu, who paid me the compliment of approaching me with this book project and who have been tremendously supportive and encouraging as I have worked on it. And as always, I am thankful for the ongoing advice and support I receive from Professor Robert Kaplan, formerly my PhD advisor and now a trusted mentor.

Preface to the Second Edition

I have been extremely grateful for the positive response to *Treatment of Error* and was excited to undertake the challenge of a new edition. Research on written corrective feedback in L2 writing and in second language acquisition has proliferated over the last decade, and an update on the literature about what continues to be a controversial subject was badly needed. Beyond simply updating the literature, though, this second edition afforded me the opportunity to further explore topics I myself have wrestled with as a scholar, researcher, teacher, and teacher educator—the growing diversity in what we call "L2 writers," the blurring boundaries between "native" and "non-native" speakers of English, the influence of genre studies and corpus linguistics on our approaches to teaching writing, and the need to move beyond "error" to "second language development" in how we approach students and their texts.

In this second edition, I have made the following changes and additions:

- Updated the literature in all chapters, especially Chapters 1–2, and substantially reordered and added to the material in those opening chapters
- Wrote an entirely new chapter (6) on academic language development
- Added a postscript on how to integrate the error treatment/language development suggestions in Chapters 4–6 into a writing class syllabus
- With an eye to the book's potential use in pedagogy courses or teacher development workshops, added discussion/analysis questions to the end of each chapter, along with a concise list of suggested further readings.

Other changes in the book are slightly less global and perhaps more subtle. For instance, I rearranged sections and added headings in some chapters to make them flow better. Also, in order to retain the book's original (popular) characteristic of being good "airplane reading," in most cases I have limited the number of in-text citations and added some key references to chapter endnotes instead. Finally, I have broadened my original conception of the audience for this book; in the first edition, I envisioned primarily, even exclusively, ESL teachers of writing courses, reading-writing courses, or integrated language skills courses that include writing. In this edition, bearing in mind the blurring of disciplinary divisions between "L1 composition" and "L2 composition," I have tried to also address the knowledge base and concerns of writing/composition instructors who were not trained primarily as ESL teachers but who nonetheless find themselves working with L2 writers in their classes. The changes that ensued were small but consistent throughout the book, for instance, speaking of "teachers of L2 writers" instead of "L2 writing teachers." I hope that this broadened vision will make the book more readily accessible to non-TESOL audiences who might be interested in the subject matter.

I should add some acknowledgments to those I made in the preface to the first edition. I have changed institutions, so I should add my thanks to my colleagues in the University Writing Program (my home department) at the University of California, Davis, as well as my own students, from whom I learn new things all the time. I am especially grateful for the ongoing encouragement and support of my editor at the University of Michigan Press, Kelly Sippell. I also want to mention my new (since the publication of the first edition) friend John Bitchener of AUT University in Auckland, New Zealand, and esteemed colleagues/friends who have been *Treatment of Error* fans, Deborah Crusan of Wright State University and Keith Folse of the University of Central Florida. I would also like to thank the co-researchers (current and former graduate students) who have worked with me most recently on new primary research on this topic: Jeffrey Brown, Hsiang (Sean) Liu, Manuel Senna, and Aparna Sinha. Finally, another shout-out to my husband, Randy Ferris; to Melissa, the kid still at home who gets neglected near deadlines; and to Winnie the Pooch, who keeps me company when I'm writing.

Contents

Chapter 1

Is Error Treatment Helpful for L2 Writers?

This book proceeds on the assumption that its readers believe in the value of corrective feedback (CF) for L2 writers and want practical, field-tested strategies for approaching what can be a daunting and frustrating task. Indeed, most of the book is devoted to the discussion and illustration of such tools. However, given the amount of discussion and controversy generated by this topic, especially over the past 15 years, we would be remiss if we did not foreground the discussion of *how* to address the treatment of error with examination of *if* and *why* we should do so. That is the goal of this first chapter.

Definitions

Two important constructs are embedded in the title of this chapter and of this book: *error* and *second language (L2) writers*. Though a casual observer might believe that both terms are self-explanatory, those immersed in the (sub)fields of second language acquisition (SLA), composition, and second language writing studies know that they are not.

Error

Both SLA and composition scholars have examined and even challenged the notion of "error" at various points in time. For example, in a classic SLA piece, Corder (1967) argued that what we term as "error" in L2 learners is actually a natural developmental stage, analogous to what children exhibit in acquiring a L1. Because nearly all children pass eventually through these stages to adult competence in the L1 without intervention, by extension, L2 errors should not be seen as problematic either. In a different line of argument, Williams (1981), writing in a mainstream composition journal, asserted that errors are primarily in the eye of the beholder and especially in the minds of writing teachers wielding red pens—in other words, we notice errors in student writing because we are looking for them, not because they are truly bothersome. In other contexts, we might not even spot them at all.

Though these lines of argument problematize the notion of error in student writing and/or how to study it, most writing instructors, especially those focused on L2 students, would counter them with the following assertions:

1. Though many L2 writing errors may indeed be developmental and may resolve themselves over time and with more exposure to the L2, not all of them will. There is considerable evidence that adult L2 learners may *fossilize*—get stuck and fail to make progress—without sufficient motivation and opportunity (including feedback and instruction) to do so.[1]

2. While many writing teachers do obsess over relatively minor points such as correct comma placement, to the extent scholars claim that *all* written error is merely a figment of a teacher-reader's overactive imagination, the argument goes too far. L2 student writers *do* produce non-target constructions that many, if not all, proficient users of the language would not only notice but identify as incorrect. Further, some of these are *global* errors, meaning that they interfere with overall text comprehensibility.[2]

Aside from the scholarly viewpoints discussed, another issue in defining "error" as it pertains to student writing is a practical one: Teachers themselves may have poorly described, even idiosyncratic notions of what constitutes an error in a given text. For example, recently I interacted with a graduate student instructor about the following sentence excerpt in a student paper: ". . . students **try and make** their essays sound fancy but end up making them confusing." She argued that ". . . try to make . . . " would be correct. I agreed that her version sounded more idiomatic and appropriate than the student's but observed that the original construction was not, in fact, grammatically incorrect. The point is that instructors can get seriously sidetracked in tinkering with students' prose to make it "sound better," when in most instances they should (a) be focusing their feedback attention on more pressing issues and (b) not be appropriating or taking over the students' texts by rewriting them.[3]

With these philosophical, theoretical, and practical questions in mind, it seems helpful for this discussion going forward to offer a concrete working definition of what we really mean by "error" in student writing:

> Errors are morphological, syntactic, and lexical forms that deviate from rules of the target language, violating the expectations of literate adult native speakers.

While there are doubtless other ways the term could be defined, this definition seems user-friendly enough as a starting point for the issues and suggestions raised in this book.

L2/Second Language Writers

Over the past 20 years, classroom practitioners and L2 writing researchers have become increasingly aware that the population of student writers has changed. Whereas early discussions of ESL/L2 writing focused primarily on the needs of international students, by the 1990s, scholars began to refer specifically to distinctions between international (visa) and immigrant/resident student writers.[4] Toward the end of the 1990s, the term *Generation 1.5* had become more familiar, especially after the publication of an edited collection entitled

Generation 1.5 Meets College Composition (Harklau, Losey, & Siegal, 1999). In the ensuing years, we have begun to speak of L2 writers as comprising at least three distinct groups (see Ferris, 2009; see also Roberge, Siegal, & Harklau, 2009):

1. **international/visa students** pursuing an education in an English-dominant country (where English is the relevant L2)
2. **resident immigrants** who arrived in the English-dominant country as adolescents or young adults
3. **the children of resident immigrants** who arrived in the English-dominant country at a very young age or who were born in the new country (i.e., the **Generation 1.5**[5] group).

Of course, even within these three subgroups of L2 writers, there is substantial diversity and complexity as to L1s and cultures represented, educational pathways (including especially how L2 literacy was acquired), legal and socioeconomic factors, and so forth. What these L2 writers do have in common is that *they all began life in homes in which the primary language was not English (or the L2).* However, what happens in the lives of individual students after these early years makes all the difference to the students' general academic progress, to their L2 literacy development, and, specific to the concerns of this book, the best ways to approach corrective feedback, or treatment of error, to facilitate their overall writing development. The following subgroup profiles briefly explore these differences, but readers should note that these are necessarily generalizations, and that individual instructors should take care to investigate the backgrounds and knowledge bases of the student writers in their own classes.

International Students

Generally speaking, international students are well educated and highly literate in their L1s. They tend to come from economically advantaged backgrounds and have often studied English (or the L2) for some years in their home countries before venturing abroad. In most cases, this L2 instruction involved formal grammar instruction and an emphasis on learning grammatical terms and rules. Reid (1998a) famously called these students "eye learners," who acquired what they know about the English language primarily through what they saw rather than through what they heard. Many English language teaching materials were designed for these students and assumed background knowledge of terms such as *verb, tense, subject, agreement,* and so on. International students often enjoy and feel comfortable with a structured approach to language instruction—which is what they are accustomed to—and want and expect their teachers to provide direct correction of all of their writing errors.

Late-Arriving Resident Immigrants

Students who arrived in the new country as adolescents or adults tend to be quite different from international students. Though both groups share the characteristics of being relative newcomers and needing to adjust to cultural and educational differences, late-arriving residents may have had interrupted L1 schooling and haphazard or even nonexistent L2 instruction. Unlike international students, they cannot necessarily draw on well-established L1 language and literacy knowledge or on a solid foundation in the L2. As this pertains to error treatment issues, they may not know formal grammar terms or rules to the extent international students probably would, if at all. However, depending on how long they have been in the new country and the amount of exposure they have had to the L2, their acquired intuitions about what "sounds right" in the L2 might help them to self-edit their writing in ways similar to what native speakers might do. For this reason, Reid (1998a) called resident immigrants "ear learners"—because their knowledge about the L2 comes primarily from what they have heard rather than what they have seen or read.

Early-Arriving or Generation 1.5 Students

In most cases, these students have lived in the new country with their immigrant parents from a very young age and have never been educated in a language other than the L2. Many, though they can speak their L1 with their parents, are not literate in that language, especially if it has a non-alphabetic writing system. Nonetheless, depending on where they went to school and what their surrounding community was like, some Generation 1.5 students may still exhibit non-native characteristics in their writing even when they reach high school or college. For example, Roberge (2002) discusses several subcategories of Generation 1.5 learners, such as *linguistic enclave* students (those who grew up in a community where nearly everyone spoke exclusively their parents' L1) and *transnational students* (those who regularly traveled back and forth between their parents' home country and new country for seasonal work and had their education interrupted). It should be apparent that these Generation 1.5 students might have different language and writing issues than those who grew up entirely in an English-dominant community with an uninterrupted education in English.

Complicating the matter further is the question of *educational pathways.* Some Generation 1.5 students may have arrived in kindergarten not knowing a word of English and, depending on the school district's philosophy and resources, may have been placed into some kind of transitional bilingual or ESL program and later mainstreamed by middle school or high school. By that point, their academic literacy development often lagged behind that of peers, and these newly mainstreamed L2 students may not have taken the most advanced English or language arts classes (Harklau, 2000; Harklau & Siegal, 2009). In a recent study of Generation 1.5 freshmen in a university ESL writing course, nearly all remembered receiving formal English grammar instruction in secondary school, but none described it as being particularly helpful or relevant to them as they completed academic writing tasks in English (Ferris et al., 2010, 2011). Like the late-arriving resident students, these early arrivals can utilize acquired intuitions about the L2—likely even better ones because of their more extended and varied exposure to the L2, especially texts—to self-correct their writing and/or to apply expert feedback. In other words, they are also ear learners under Reid's dichotomy, but their ears may be better attuned to the L2 than those of the late-arriving group.

This brief overview of different L2 writer subgroups leads to at least two important observations. First, instructors cannot apply a one-size-fits-all strategy to the treatment of error in student writing. Different students will have varying types of knowledge (formal grammar knowledge vs. acquired intuition) about the L2, so *approaches to written feedback and to classroom instruction about writing errors will have to be tailored accordingly.* We will discuss this in much more detail in Chapters 4 and 5. Second, for effective treatment of error, *it is critically important that instructors take time to get to know their students at the beginning of a writing course—* their backgrounds, the amount of formal knowledge they have about language, and the particular strengths and weaknesses in writing that they bring into the class. We will discuss this point further in Chapters 3 and 5 as well.

Perspectives on Error Correction

Having defined some basic terms (*error* and *L2 writer*), we turn briefly now to summarizing the history of error correction as it has been practiced in language teaching, in composition courses, and in the specialized arena of L2 writing.

A Brief History

Over the short but eventful history of teaching composition to L2 writers, teachers' and theorists' views of the importance of grammar, error correction, and accuracy have undergone several shifts. Writing for L2 students was, until the 1970s, primarily perceived as language practice, to manipulate grammatical forms or to utilize newly learned vocabulary items (Ferris & Hedgcock, 2005; Johns, 1990; Raimes, 1991; Silva, 1990). Writing in L2 classes typically consisted of "controlled," or "guided," composition activities in which students, for instance, would write a paragraph about "what I did yesterday" in order to practice the use of the past tense or would change the nouns in an already constructed paragraph from singular to plural forms. Influenced by theories of behavioral psychology and structural linguistics on second language teaching, teachers gave a great deal of attention to students' accuracy, or lack thereof, constantly correcting all errors so that no bad habits would form. In addition, teachers carefully taught students grammatical forms and rules assumed to be problematic because of contrasts with students' native languages.[6] Thus, error correction and grammar instruction were major, perhaps even the primary, components of writing instruction in L2 classes.

In the 1970s, composition practitioners and theorists began to focus on writers themselves and on the processes they used to construct texts. This led to a major paradigm shift that had great implications for both L1 and L2 writing classes in the United States. Rather than emphasizing correct forms for essays, paragraphs, and sentences, teachers and students were encouraged to focus on discovering ideas, drafting, revising, working collaboratively, and sharing successes. Though process approach advocates gave lip-service to the continued importance of accuracy in students' finished products, attention to grammar was left to the end of the process (or the "editing" phase). Generally, it was assumed that if students were engaged in writing about topics they had chosen themselves and were empowered to make decisions about the shaping and polishing of their own texts, final products would improve as a natural consequence of a more enlightened process.[7] Since both teachers and students found it more stimulating and less tedious to focus on ideas than on accuracy, composition instruction entered a period of "benign neglect" of errors and grammar teaching (Ferris, 1995c).

As process pedagogy entered L2 writing classes, some scholars almost immediately began to express concerns about the neglect of accuracy issues and its effects on ESL writers. An early piece, entitled "Meanwhile, back in the real world…" (Eskey, 1983), reminded us that the ability to correct errors is crucial in many settings and that students' accuracy will not magically improve all by itself. Similar concerns were raised by Horowitz (1986), who also pointed out the limitations of the process approach for teaching ESL writers to function in real academic settings. Other scholars began to note the inherent differences between L1 and L2 writers and to suggest that pedagogical suggestions designed for native speakers needed to be critically re-evaluated in light of these distinctions (e.g., Leki, 1990; Silva, 1988, 1993; Zhang, 1995). Though L1 student writing is obviously not error-free, the errors made by L2 writers tend to be different in quantity and nature (see Chapter 3 for more discussion of this point). Because L2 students, in addition to being developing writers, are still in the process of acquiring the L2 lexicon and morphological and syntactic systems, they often need distinct and additional intervention from their writing teachers to bridge these gaps and develop strategies for finding, correcting, and avoiding errors.

Second Language Acquisition and Its Implications for Error Correction

As most L2 teachers and learners are only too aware, second language acquisition (SLA) takes time and occurs in stages. Though SLA research is not conclusive as to specific orders and stages of acquisition, several generalizations have emerged[8]:

- It takes **a significant amount of time to acquire an L2**, and even more when the learner is attempting to use the language for academic purposes.
- Depending on learner characteristics, most notably, age of first exposure to the L2, **some acquirers may never attain native-like control** of various aspects of the L2.
- **SLA occurs in stages**. Vocabulary, morphology, phonology, and syntax may all represent separately occurring stages of acquisition.

- As learners go through various stages of acquisition of different elements of the L2, **they will make errors reflective of their SLA processes**. These errors may be caused by inappropriate transference of L1 patterns and/ or by incomplete knowledge of the L2. Written errors made by adult L2 acquirers are therefore often quite different from those made by native speakers.

These insights from SLA research have several practical implications for teachers of L2 writers. First, it is unrealistic to expect that L2 writers' production will be error-free or that even when it is, that it will "sound" like that of monolingual English speakers (Valdés, 1992). Second, because SLA takes time, we should not expect students' accuracy to improve overnight. Third, and most important for the purposes of this book, L2 student writers need (a) a focus on different linguistic issues or error patterns than native speakers do; (b) feedback or error correction that is tailored to their linguistic knowledge and experience; and (c) instruction that is sensitive to their unique linguistic gaps and needs for strategy training, including not only strategies for finding, fixing, and avoiding errors but also for continued development of language structures that will strengthen their writing across a variety of tasks and genres.

Challenges to Error Correction in L2 Writing Classes

As already noted, the advent of the process approach in L1 and L2 writing instruction in the 1970s–1980s led to a decreased focus on student error. Since then, a number of scholars have questioned the appropriateness of this trend, some conservatively noting that L2 writers may be distinct enough from L1 writers to merit different pedagogical strategies (e.g., Carson & Nelson, 1994; Leki, 1990; Silva, 1993; Zhang, 1995), others taking stronger stances, arguing that non-interventionist teacher strategies have been "cruelly unfair to diverse students" (Johns, 1995, p. 182) or have produced adults with years of U.S. English education, even at the college/university level, who cannot function in either academic or workplace settings (Scarcella, 1996, 2003). The resulting renewed interest in error correction, grammar instruction, and editing strategy training for L2 student writers can be observed in the publication of "how-to" articles, chapters, and books for teachers as well as editing textbooks for ESL student writers[9] and sections in mainstream composition textbooks dedicated to ESL editing issues (e.g., Lunsford, 2009).

Despite—or perhaps because of—this renewed interest in grammar for ESL writers, John Truscott, in an essay published in 1996 in *Language Learning,* argued for the abandonment of grammar correction in L2 writing classes. Truscott claimed that there was no convincing research evidence that error correction ever helps student writers, that error correction as typically practiced overlooks SLA insights about how different aspects of language are acquired, and that there are practical problems related to teachers' and students' ability and willingness to give and receive error correction. He concluded that error correction was not only *useless* to student writers but that it was actually *harmful* in that it diverted time and energy away from more productive aspects of writing instruction. In a number of follow-up papers between 1996 and 2009, many of which were responses to other authors' challenges to his thesis and/or new primary research on error correction, Truscott has continued to strongly assert his position (see Truscott, 1999, 2004, 2007, 2009; Truscott & Hsu, 2008).

As I have noted elsewhere (Ferris, 2010), it is interesting and even ironic that a paper that called for the end of the ubiquitous pedagogical practice of corrective feedback to L2 writers in fact led to widespread renewed interest in the topic on the part of both researchers and practitioners. In the past 15 years, a number of researchers have examined the question of whether corrective feedback is helpful for L2 student writers, along with a variety of related subquestions. Though there are many research questions that could productively still be examined, these recent research efforts have added considerably to our knowledge, not only about *whether* teachers of L2 writers should continue to provide error feedback to their students but especially about *how* they might go about doing so. These lines of research and their findings are described in some detail in Chapter 2; here we will simply summarize the primary arguments in answer to the question posed by the title of this chapter: Is error treatment helpful for L2 writers?

Arguments for Continued Error Treatment

Error Feedback Helps Students Revise and Edit Their Texts

Studies examining the short-term effects of error feedback on revisions of existing texts have consistently demonstrated that error feedback can help students to improve the accuracy of those texts.[10] That these findings are clear and consistent is not controversial. However, this body of work has been criticized because it does not demonstrate that students' ability to make revisions on existing texts transfers to improved accuracy and effectiveness in writing over time (Ellis et al., 2008; Truscott, 1996, 2007; Truscott & Hsu, 2008). Nonetheless, it certainly may be argued that long-term development is unlikely without observable short-term improvement, at least in the ability to attend to and correct errors when pointed out by teachers (Ferris, 2004, 2010; Sachs & Polio, 2007). Thus, this small but growing research base, while it does not answer all theoretical questions related to error correction, should not be ignored as meaningless, either.

Error Feedback Leads to Accuracy Gains over Time

In recent years, a number of researchers have taken up Truscott's challenge to study the effects of corrective feedback on written accuracy over time (i.e., on new texts rather than only revised ones). Using a controlled quasi-experimental approach with a pre-test/post-test/delayed post-test design, several studies have consistently showed that when corrective feedback was limited to several discrete categories (e.g., definite and indefinite articles), students receiving error feedback substantially outperformed those who received no feedback on both post-tests and delayed post-tests.[11] Longitudinal studies of error feedback in classroom settings also yielded positive effects for error feedback, but in some cases the studies did not include a no-feedback control group, and in others, the results were mixed across individual students, type/timing of writing task, and error type(s) considered.[12] The most recent study (van Beuningen et al., 2011) was also the most substantial, examining the effects of corrective feedback given to hundreds of student writers on both revisions and new texts and considering a wider variety of error categories than had earlier studies. While there is still a range of questions that could productively be explored in further research (see Ferris, 2010, for specific suggestions), these studies, most of which have been completed within the past decade, have provided a great deal of helpful information both about the impact of corrective feedback and on ways to approach it pedagogically (see Chapters 2 and 4).[13]

Students and Teachers Value Error Feedback

As noted by a number of researchers, students value teacher feedback on their errors and think that it helps them to improve their writing.[14] Truscott (1996) anticipated this argument and responded that "students believe in correction . . . but that does not mean that teachers should give it to them" (p. 359) and that teachers should, rather than giving in to this student desire, help them adjust to the absence of grammar correction (see Truscott, 1999). However, given the unquestioned (even by Truscott) strength of student demand for error correction, the possible harm to student motivation and confidence in their instructors may far outweigh any possible damage that could come to them from providing error feedback. Most teachers of L2 writers instructors know that were they to refuse to give any error feedback or grammar instruction, it would cause a rift between them and their students. This potential negative outcome is not one that may be dismissed lightly nor overcome easily.

In addition to the strongly held views of student writers, the fact is that most teachers at least implicitly believe in the importance of error feedback and provide it consistently to their students. This is true despite the fact that researchers and theorists in both SLA and composition studies have been questioning the practice for decades. As recently as 2006, Santa, whose monograph traces the history of error treatment in composition, noted with some bewilderment teachers' "recalcitrant response to error in student writing" (p. 104). Santa's observation is supported by a range of recent studies of teachers' feedback practices, all of which clearly demonstrate that today's classroom instructors remain committed to providing error feedback (among other things) to their student writers.[15] If teachers are providing corrective feedback to their student writers, perhaps it is most important for researchers to turn their primary attention to discovering the most effective ways for them to do so (Bruton, 2009; Evans et al., 2010; Hartshorn et al., 2010).[16]

Written Accuracy Is Important in the Real World

Finally, instructors need to work at finding the best ways to help their students become "independent self-editors" of their own work (Bates, Lane, & Lange, 1993; Ferris, 1995c). This is because accuracy matters in the world outside of the writing class. Both anecdotal and research evidence suggest that at least in some settings, university professors and employers find language errors in writing distracting and stigmatizing.[17] Student writers' lexical, morphological, and syntactic accuracy is important because a lack of precision may both interfere with the comprehensibility of their message (or ideas) and may mark them as inadequate users of the language. Writing instructors surely have some responsibility to equip their students with the knowledge, strategies, and resources they will need to function effectively outside of the writing classroom (Gray-Rosendale, 1998; Johns, 1995; Scarcella, 1996, 2003). Though research may still be inconclusive as to the best ways to accomplish these goals, it seems clear that if teachers abdicate this responsibility altogether, students are unlikely to make adequate progress in editing skills and overall accuracy.[18]

Concluding Thoughts

It is important to acknowledge that the research data base on error correction and grammar instruction is incomplete (as it is in many, if not most, areas of ESL teaching) and that scholars have raised various objections to the practice of error correction in writing classes. That said, our knowledge about this ubiquitous yet controversial pedagogical practice has evolved a great deal even since the first edition of this book was published in 2002. For the reasons outlined in the previous section, the remainder of this book is devoted to identifying ways in which teachers can prepare themselves and their students to focus on accuracy in writing most effectively.

Questions for Discussion and Application

1. As a student writer (whether in L1 or L2), have you ever received corrective feedback from a teacher on language errors? If so, what is your opinion about the benefits or drawbacks of the practice?
2. As a teacher or prospective teacher, have you ever considered the question raised in the chapter, "Is corrective feedback helpful for L2 writers?" or have you just assumed that it is (or is not)?

3. What do you think of the two early theoretical perspectives about error discussed in this chapter: (1) Error is simply a developmental stage that learners will naturally pass through and (2) Errors are created in the minds of teachers who are conditioned to look for them? As a writer, learner, or teacher, do either of these perspectives make sense to you? Why or why not?

4. In a now-famous paper, Truscott (1996) argued that error correction for L2 writers is useless, harmful, and should be abandoned. As a possible follow-up to reading this chapter, read Truscott's article and a few of his later papers, if available (see the References section at the end of this book for titles). Which of his arguments (if any) do you find most interesting or convincing? Which of his arguments (if any) do you question most?

5. The final section of this chapter outlines a series of arguments in favor of the practice of corrective feedback for L2 writers. Choose the one you find most interesting, and read one or more of the studies cited in that section, if available. Did you find the evidence presented in that study (studies) convincing, and does it (do they) truly support the assertions in this chapter? Why or why not?

6. This chapter—and indeed the entire book—is based on the premise that there is enough evidence to believe that error treatment can be helpful under the right conditions and that researchers and teachers should focus on the best ways to provide it. Do you agree with this premise, or do you feel that researchers should continue to try to prove that corrective feedback is effective—and if so, should teachers stop giving error feedback in the meantime?

Further Reading

These sources will help you go further in understanding the major themes developed in this chapter. Complete bibliographic information is provided in the References section at the end of the book. The list is presented alphabetically rather than chronologically or thematically.

Beason, L. (2001).
Bitchener, J., & Knoch, U. (2010a).
Ferris, D.R. (2004).
Hartshorn, J.K., Evans, N.W., Merrill, P.F., Sudweeks, R.R., Strong-Krause, D., & Anderson, N.J. (2010).
Leki, I. (1991).
Montgomery, J.L., & Baker, W. (2007).
Reid, J. (1998a).
Roberge, M.M. (2002).
Truscott, J. (1996).
Williams, J.M. (1981).

CHAPTER 1 NOTES

1. For SLA views on learner noticing and needs for negative evidence, see, e.g., Long (1996); Schmidt (1994).

2. For discussions of the "global/local" distinction, see Bates, Lane, & Lange, 1993; Burt & Kiparsky, 1972; Hendrickson, 1980.

3. There are some possible exceptions to this general statement. For instance, if a student is highly proficient and not making (m)any other types of language errors, the teacher might want to work intentionally with the writer on strategies for elevating style and/or using idiomatic expressions appropriately. See Chapter 6 for more ideas along this line. Also, if the student is in the final stages of producing an important text for external readers (e.g., an admissions committee for a graduate program or an application for employment), the teacher may wish to give more precise stylistic feedback at that point.

4. For discussions of differences between international and resident student writers, see, e.g., Bosher & Rowekamp, 1998; Ferris, 1999b; Leki, 1992; Matsuda, 2006; Matsuda & Matsuda, 2009; Reid, 1998a, 1998b.

5. *Generation 1.5* is a term taken from Korean to apply to Korean-American immigrants' children (Park, 1999; Roberge, 2002). The term refers to their "in-between status," stemming from the fact that "their experiences, characteristics, and educational needs may lie somewhere between those of *first-generation* adult immigrants and the U.S.-born *second-generation* children of immigrants" (Roberge, 2002, pp. 107–108).

6. For discussions of contrastive analysis, see, e.g., Eckman (1977) and Wardhaugh (1970).

7. For discussions of process writing in L1/L2 composition, see, e.g., Elbow (1973); Sommers (1980, 1982); Zamel (1982).

8. SLA researchers who have addressed these topics include Collier (1987, 1989); Corder (1967); Krashen (1982); Truscott (1996); and Valdés (1992).

9. How-to materials include Bates, Lane, & Lange, 1993; Ferris, 1995c, 2002, 2003, 2008; Ferris & Hedgcock, 2005; Frodesen, 1991; Frodesen & Holten, 2003. Student editing textbooks include Ascher, 1993; Folse, Solomon, & Smith-Palinkas, 2003; Fox, 1992; Lane & Lange, 1999. An example of a handbook is Raimes, 2004.

10. "Revision studies" include Ashwell, 2000; Fathman & Whalley, 1990; Ferris, 2006; Ferris & Roberts, 2001; Truscott & Hsu, 2008.

11. Longitudinal controlled studies include Bitchener & Knoch, 2010a, 2010b; Bitchener, Young, & Cameron, 2005; Ellis et al., 2008; Sheen, 2007; and van Beuningan et al., in press.

12. Longitudinal classroom studies include Chandler, 2003; Ferris, 1995a, 2006; Ferris et al., 2010; Foin & Lange, 2007; Haswell, 1983.

13. For more in-depth summary and analysis of the studies discussed here, see Bitchener and Ferris (2012, Ch. 3–4); Bitchener (2008); and Ferris (2003, 2004, 2010). For possible counterarguments, see especially Truscott (2007) and Guénette (2007).

14. For studies on student views of error feedback, see Cohen, 1987; Cohen & Cavalcanti, 1990; Enginarlar, 1993; Ferris, 1995b, 2006; Ferris & Roberts, 2001; Hedgcock & Lefkowitz, 1994, 1996; Leki, 1991; Radecki & Swales, 1988; Saito, 1994.

15. For studies of teacher views and practices on feedback, see Ferris, et al., 2011; Ferris, Liu, & Rabie, 2011; Lee, 2008, 2009; Lunsford & Lunsford, 2008; Montgomery & Baker, 2007.

16. Some would counterargue that students (Truscott, 1996, 1999) and teachers (Williams, 1981) have been socialized into erroneous beliefs about the potential of error correction and, thus, the fact that both groups value the practice constitutes no real case for continuing it. There are two possible responses to this point. One is that if teachers and students believe that error correction helps student writers, they may have valid firsthand experience

that causes them to hold this view—in the case of students, because they can point to ways in which corrective feedback has helped them individually, and in the case of teachers, because they can point to sustained improvement on the part of at least some of their students. The other response is that if teachers are going to resist theorists' attempts to persuade them to stop giving corrective feedback (and history suggests that they *will* resist it), we should focus instead on finding ways to make the feedback process as valuable as possible. Research findings on the effects of corrective feedback, while not completely conclusive, do provide enough evidence to suggest that under the right conditions, it will help at least some students over time.

17. "Error gravity" studies include Beason, 2001; Hairston, 1981; Janopolous, 1992; Santos, 1988; Vann, Lorenz, & Meyer, 1991; Vann, Meyer, & Lorenz, 1984; Wall & Hull, 1989; see also Shaughnessy, 1977.

18. Even Truscott (1999) noted that there might be a place for teaching students self-editing strategies to improve their own writing—it was, rather, the role of teacher corrective feedback that he questioned.

Chapter 2

Research on Corrective Feedback in L2 Writing

As discussed in Chapter 1, there is disagreement and even controversy among writing specialists and SLA theorists as to the nature and very existence of "error," and as to whether any classroom intervention, such as teacher feedback and formal grammar instruction, can help students to improve in written accuracy over time. The purpose of this chapter, therefore, is to look at this debate more carefully by synthesizing and critically analyzing the various strands of research available on the topic of error treatment for L2 student writers. It concludes by summarizing what we know at this point and for which questions we have inadequate evidence and by outlining a possible classroom research agenda for writing teachers and scholars.

The review is structured to respond to several key questions and their related subpoints, which are outlined in Figure 2.1.

Effects of Corrective Feedback on Student Writing

Adequacy of Teacher Feedback

In discussing the effects of teacher error correction, it is first necessary to address a charge that has been leveled by several researchers and reviewers: that the feedback given by teachers is incomplete, idiosyncratic, erratic, and inaccurate.[1] Cohen

1. *What are the effects of teacher error correction on student writing?*
   - Do writing teachers give accurate and complete feedback on students' errors?
   - Do students attend to teacher feedback and attempt to utilize it in revisions of their texts?
   - Do students who receive teacher feedback on their errors make accurate changes in their revisions?
   - Do students who receive error feedback improve in written accuracy over time?
   - Does it matter what types of feedback students receive (e.g., direct or indirect, coded or uncoded)?
   - Are certain types of error more "treatable" by means of error feedback than others?

2. *What are the effects of other types of classroom intervention on the accuracy of student writing?*
   - Does all error feedback need to be written?
   - Does in-class grammar instruction help students to improve their writing?
   - Does required revision after receiving feedback facilitate student progress?
   - Does maintenance of error logs or charts help students to become more accurate over time?

3. *What are students' views and perceptions about error treatment in their writing?*
   - Do L2 student writers value error feedback, or do they resent it and find it discouraging and demotivating?
   - Do students value feedback on errors as much as feedback on other aspects of writing (ideas, organization)?
   - What specific feedback styles or mechanisms do students prefer (e.g., selective or comprehensive, direct or indirect, etc.)?

4. *What are directions for further research on error treatment?*
   - What methodological issues need to be considered?
   - What questions need additional investigation?

Figure 2.1   Issues and Questions to Be Reviewed

and Cavalcanti (1990) conducted a case study analysis in which they analyzed the feedback given by one teacher to three students—a high performer, an intermediate performer, and a low performer—in each of three distinct settings (three teachers and nine student writers in total). While they did not explicitly examine the accuracy of teacher error correction, they did note that the different teachers "only dealt with approximately half the issues that could have been dealt with" or "avoided or overlooked over twice as many problems as she commented on" (1990, pp. 160–161). In other words, the teachers' feedback was not *comprehensive*: It did not address all of the language issues independently identified by the researchers. However, the authors also noted that their design did not include a means to assess whether such omissions were "a conscious choice . . . an oversight, or the result of lack of knowledge about that issue" (p. 173). Though Cohen and Cavalcanti's study was quite small, similar findings were recently reported in a large nationwide study of composition teachers' error feedback (Lunsford & Lunsford, 2008).

Cohen and Robbins (1976) followed the progress of three ESL college students over a semester, examining a variety of student texts, to assess (among other things) whether teacher error correction appeared to influence student progress in accuracy over time. They reported that "the corrections did not seem to have any significant effect on student errors. But a closer look at the whole correction process suggested that *the specific process of correction was at fault, rather than correction in general*" (1976, p. 50, emphasis added). In particular, corrections were given at various times by three different instructors (the main instructor and two volunteer aides), leading to a possible lack of consistency. While it certainly seems possible and even likely that having three different people, two of whom were "volunteer aides," may have led to inconsistent or faulty error correction, no specific data are presented in support of this claim.

Unlike the two small-scale case studies by Cohen and his co-authors, Zamel's (1985) study of teacher commentary on student writing considered a more substantial sample of subjects—15 teachers, each responding to three or more students, on a total of 105 ESL student papers, not including revisions (p. 85). In a now-famous and often-cited quote, Zamel reported that "ESL writing teachers misread student texts, are inconsistent in their reactions, make arbitrary corrections, write contradictory comments . . . [and] overwhelmingly view themselves as language teachers rather than writing teachers; they attend primarily to surface features of writing . . ." (p. 86). Unfortunately, though Zamel went on in the article to provide numerous clear examples and illustrations of her claims about teacher feedback, she did not provide any information about her method of analysis nor any statistics to indicate whether the examples she provided were indeed representative of the entire sample of 105 student papers responded to by 15 different writing instructors. As in the case of Cohen and Robbins' (1976) study, while the assertions made by the authors seem believable, they were not well supported by actual data (at least not as reported in the article).

More recently, in a semester-long study, Ferris (2006) examined both the accuracy and completeness of error feedback given by three university ESL teachers to 92 ESL writers. In all, 146 texts and 5,707 errors marked by teachers were analyzed. It was found that the error corrections made by the teachers were correct in about 89 percent of the instances, with 3.6 percent judged as "incorrect" and 7 percent judged as "unnecessary." In a separate analysis of 110 unmarked papers from the sample, it was found that the teachers marked more than 83 percent of the errors identified independently by two researchers. In sum, while it may well be true that some L2 writing instructors are inaccurate and inconsistent in providing error feedback, there are as yet no studies that support this claim empirically and only one that refutes this charge.

Researchers in two different contexts have also examined the issue of whether teachers' written feedback (including error correction) matches their perceptions and their beliefs. Montgomery and Baker (2007), who studied teachers in an intensive ESL program in the United States, found that teachers gave much more form-focused feedback than they thought they did and that their responding behaviors at times did not match up to their stated philosophies about feedback or to the ongoing training they were receiving. Lee (2008, 2009) studied secondary English teachers in Hong Kong, finding "mismatches" between teacher beliefs and practices about corrective feedback, which some instructors attributed to external pressures (from government, school administrators, parents, or students themselves).

In studies of corrective feedback in L2 writing, the "teacher variable" is usually either ignored or removed altogether from the research design. In studies where actual teacher feedback is analyzed, it is often assumed that teacher correction is accurate, comprehensive, and consistent. If more than one teacher is involved, it is presumed that the teachers are all giving feedback in the same ways and with the same degrees of quality.[2] The study by Ferris (2006) is an exception to this generalization, but only by accident: The three teachers involved in the study had agreed to give comprehensive correction using a system of 15 standard error codes, but when the researchers began analyzing the data, they found that the instructors had in fact deviated from the agreed-upon system. Thus, a part of the data analysis involved developing descriptions of what teachers had *actually* done rather than what they were *supposed to* have done. In other studies, the teacher variable is removed from the equation because the researchers themselves provide the error feedback. While this latter approach no doubt yields more reliable findings about the effects of such feedback, it provides little insight as to how practicing classroom teachers approach the challenging task of giving corrective feedback to their students.

Student Uptake of Error Feedback

Teacher Correction and Timed Student Revision

Another criticism of teacher error correction and of written feedback in general is that students do not pay attention to it (Cohen, 1987; Ferris, Liu, & Rabie, 2011; Truscott, 1996). Several studies of error correction have examined this issue at least indirectly using a range of research designs. Haswell (1983) studied the effects in his freshman composition classes of his "minimal marking" approach,[3] finding that students corrected (in 15 minutes or fewer) more than 61 percent of errors marked by the teacher. Though Haswell's students most likely were all or nearly all monolingual English speakers, similar findings were reported with ESL university students in a study by Ferris and Roberts (2001).[4] In Frantzen and Rissel (1987), 22 students in a university Spanish class were given ten minutes to correct errors that had been marked by the instructor/researcher, with "an incentive of a slightly improved grade given to those who corrected at least 75 percent of their corrected errors" (p. 93). The subjects successfully corrected nearly 92 percent of all of the errors marked. However, a controlled experimental situation in which direct incentives are given for editing may not demonstrate what students might do with teacher corrections under more naturalistic circumstances.

Teacher Correction Followed by Out-of-Class Revision

In a longitudinal classroom study of 1,467 teacher comments on 110 pairs—first drafts and revisions—of student papers, Ferris (1997) found that of 109 comments made specifically about grammar issues, only 15 (14 percent) were left unaddressed by the students in their revisions. Finally, in the study by Ferris (2006), it was found that of 5,707 errors marked by teachers, students attempted corrections in 90.7 percent of the cases. (Of the errors, 9.3 percent were coded "no change," meaning that the identical error reappeared in the student revision.)[5] In short, based on the limited evidence available, when student writers received expert feedback on their writing and were required to revise it (whether under timed, supervised conditions or at home), they indeed attended to most teacher feedback and tried to apply it. Where they did not, a recently completed, longitudinal multiple–case study of 10 L2 writers (Ferris et al., 2010) provides some possible clues as to why. In several interviews following feedback and revision cycles, the students reported that they would not address corrections if (a) they did not have enough time to go over them carefully;

(b) they did not understand the error codes, terms, or symbols used to describe the errors; or (c) they did not know how to correct the problem even when it was called to their attention.

The Influence of Error Feedback on Student Revision

A related question is whether students make correct revisions on papers in response to teacher feedback. The evidence on this question that exists to this point is fairly conclusive: Though there is variation across error type, individual students, and teacher feedback mechanisms, student writers have generally been successful in producing more accurate revisions in response to error feedback. As already mentioned, the subjects in Frantzen and Rissel's (1987) study were able to self-correct nearly 92 percent of the errors marked by the teacher. In Fathman and Whalley's (1990) study, 100 percent of the students who received grammar feedback received higher grammar scores on their revisions (Table 2, p. 184). In Ferris's (1997) study, 73 percent of the grammar-focused teacher comments led to successful changes in the student revisions—notable because these were verbal comments made in the margins or in endnotes, as opposed to at the point of error in the text. In the study by Ferris (2006), students made successful edits of about 80 percent of the errors marked by their teachers.

Three studies published since 2000 compared revision success rates between students who received error feedback and control groups of students who were asked to revise/edit their papers on their own with no feedback (Ashwell, 2000; Ferris & Roberts, 2001; Truscott & Hsu, 2008). In all three studies, the treatment group(s) significantly outperformed the control group on the revision tasks. As noted in Chapter 1, these studies have been criticized because the effects of correction were not further measured by examining the accuracy of new student texts. Nonetheless, as to the question of whether between-draft error feedback helps L2 writers to successfully revise their texts in progress, the answer thus far is clearly yes.

Effects of Error Feedback on Student Accuracy over Time

While it is interesting to observe whether students attend to and successfully incorporate teacher error feedback into papers they immediately revise, it is arguably more important to assess whether such intervention actually helps students to acquire correct language forms and improve their self-editing strategies, as measured through improved written accuracy over time. One of Truscott's (1996) major criticisms of the existing body of research on error correction in L2 writing was that there was little evidence that teacher feedback facilitates improvement of student writing in the long run. In response to this observation, a number of researchers have in recent years completed studies carefully designed to examine longer-term effects of written corrective feedback. As I have noted elsewhere (Ferris, 2010), these studies can be subdivided between experimental designs conducted mostly by SLA researchers and classroom investigations by L2 writing researchers.

SLA Studies of Written Corrective Feedback

Researchers in this tradition have usually been influenced by studies of oral corrective feedback and its impact on learner acquisition. These studies[6] have the following characteristics in common:

1. There is a pre-test (original text)/post-test (new text)/delayed post-test (new text written later) design.
2. There is always a control group receiving no error feedback for comparison purposes.
3. The types of errors marked on the pre-tests are narrowly drawn and limited in number.
4. The errors are marked by the researcher(s) rather than by the classroom teachers.
5. The texts are produced under timed conditions for the purposes of the research; they are not a regular part of the language/writing class.

When measured under these conditions, the effects of error feedback have been robust: In all cases, the treatment groups significantly outperformed the control group in producing more accurate texts on post-tests, and the effects persisted over time, ranging from a few weeks to ten months (Bitchener & Knoch, 2010a). Though the studies differed from one another as to error types measured and the ways in which error feedback was given, the body of work as a whole demonstrates that error feedback on these targeted forms can improve students' written accuracy over time.

Classroom Studies of the Effects of Corrective Feedback over Time

As I have noted elsewhere (Ferris, 2004), there are practical barriers to designing studies in which a group of student writers receives no error feedback over a substantial period of time while others do receive it. Administrators or research review boards may forbid such designs, students may protest them, and teachers themselves may feel ethically constrained from conducting or participating in these studies. As a result, some researchers have found creative ways to set up contrasts. For instance, in Kepner's (1991) study of college-level students of Spanish, she gave feedback on content to some students and feedback on grammar to others; all students received feedback, but it was focused on different issues. In Chandler's (2003) study of college ESL writers, she circumvented the control group problem by having some students revise their papers immediately after receiving corrective feedback while others (the "controls") did not do so until many weeks later.

Other researchers have simply measured the longitudinal effects of corrective feedback by comparing students' accuracy at the beginning and end of a treatment period, perhaps varying the methods of feedback provided to different groups of students but without attempting to include a no-feedback control group. For example, Lalande (1982) compared foreign language students' writing progress over time when one group received comprehensive direct correction while the other received selective indirect correction.[7] Ferris (1995a) tracked

30 students over a semester; their most frequent patterns of error were targeted for them at the beginning of the course, and their progress in reducing or eliminating those errors was traced in both in-class and out-of-class writing. Ferris (2006) examined 55 students' papers at the beginning and end of a semester, measuring their progress in five broad error categories that had been marked throughout the term. Results of such studies have been mixed, with researchers generally reporting some progress in accuracy by nearly all students, but also finding that individual students had differing rates of improvement and that progress also varied according to error types.[8] There is no evidence from these studies that students regressed or were otherwise harmed by the corrective feedback they received. However, critics would note that absent a no-feedback control group in these studies, it is hard to argue that the error feedback (and not, say, additional writing practice or exposure to the L2) is responsible for the progress measured over time. It is also important to note that available longitudinal classroom studies varied from one another on just about every research parameter imaginable—subject characteristics, duration of treatment, types of student texts and teacher feedback being considered, and analysis methods (see Ferris, 2003, 2004, for more detailed discussions of this point).

Research on Feedback Approaches

As noted by Truscott (1996, 1999) and in Chapter 1, most researchers and teachers appear to begin with the presumption that error correction is helpful to students and focus primarily on trying to identify the most effective mechanisms and strategies for giving error feedback. Thus, rather than contrasting the writing of students receiving no error feedback with the texts of those who do, many studies of error correction instead examine the effects of varying types of feedback on student accuracy. The most important dichotomies in written corrective feedback discussed in the literature are (a) the effects of focused and unfocused feedback and (b) the effects of direct and indirect feedback.

Focused and Unfocused Feedback

Though the terms *focused* and *unfocused* have been characterized in various ways by researchers over the years, they essentially distinguish between feedback that is targeted to specific error types or patterns and correction of any and all problems observed in the text without a preconceived feedback approach in mind. For example, in some studies, the researchers provide feedback on a discrete number of predetermined error categories, such as articles or prepositions. The types and numbers of error categories have varied widely, from only two or three narrowly drawn categories (Bitchener, Young, & Cameron, 2005; Bitchener & Knoch, 2009, 2010a, 2010b; Ellis et al., 2008; Sheen, 2007) to five to seven broadly drawn categories such as verbs, noun endings, or sentence structure (e.g., Ferris & Roberts, 2001; van Beuningan et al., in press) to a broad range of as many as 15 categories (e.g., Ferris, 2006). Another approach to research with focused feedback starts with the students' most frequent error patterns, as demonstrated on a piece of writing completed at the beginning of the course, providing systematic feedback (and supplementary instruction) on those error patterns, and tracking students' progress over time (e.g., Ferris, 1995a; Ferris et al., 2010). In both types of research, the principle or assumption is the same:

> . . . a comprehensive, yet vague approach to written CF, compared with selective treatment of targeted error types, is less likely to yield empirically robust findings and be pedagogically effective. It only makes sense that students would utilize written CF more effectively for long-term language acquisition and writing development when there are fewer, clearer error types on which to focus attention. (Ferris, 2010, p. 182)

In particular, it makes intuitive sense to instructors that students will benefit more from correction if they receive precise information about the types of errors they make, the relative frequency of those errors, and the progress (or lack thereof) that they are making than they will from a random collection of scattered error markings on a broad range of linguistic issues. Only the most competent and motivated student writers might actually study such unfocused correction and draw productive generalizations from it that might faciliate their future writing. In most cases, the students will simply look at it (or not) and forget it.

While the case for focused correction sounds compelling, there are two important counterarguments to mention. First, only one study to date (Ellis et al., 2008) has directly compared the effects of focused and unfocused corrective feedback (on student writers' accuracy in using English indefinite articles), finding no difference in outcomes between the two treatment groups, though both outperformed the no-feedback control group.

Second, several L2 writing researchers have observed that the selection of a limited number of error types for feedback may not give student writers the information they need about the broad(er) range of errors they may make: While students may make progress on the two or three error types focused on in corrective feedback, what about all the others? As noted by Ferris (2010), we do not really know what the "optimal" number of error types to treat at one time might be—two? five? ten? Further, as argued by Hartshorn et al. (2010) and Evans et al. (2010), in real-world writing, a high degree of accuracy is expected, and student writers need to learn how to edit *all* of their errors, not simply the few patterns picked out for them by teachers or researchers (see also Ferris, 2010). Thus, a comprehensive approach to error feedback, even if it is relatively unfocused, may better serve the students' long-term instrumental objectives better than a focused, selective approach. We will discuss specific options for these feedback choices in more detail in Chapter 4.

Direct and Indirect Feedback

When instructors provide the correct linguistic form for students—word, morpheme, phrase, rewritten sentence, deleted word(s) or morpheme(s)—this is referred to as *direct* feedback. If students are revising or rewriting their papers after receiving teacher feedback, they are expected merely to transcribe the teacher's suggested corrections into their texts. *Indirect* feedback, on the other hand, occurs when the teacher indicates that an error has been made but leaves it to the student writer to solve the problem and correct the error.[9] It has been argued that indirect feedback is more helpful to student writers in most cases because it leads to greater cognitive engagement, reflection, and problem-solving (Lalande, 1982; see also Bates, Lane, & Lange, 1993; Ferris, 1995c; Ferris & Hedgcock, 2005; Reid, 1998b). Possible exceptions might include instances in which the error in question is complex and idiosyncratic (Ferris, 1999a; Ferris & Roberts, 2001) or when student writers are not sufficiently advanced in L2 proficiency to self-correct errors even when pointed out to them (Brown, 2007; Ferris & Hedgcock, 2005; Frodesen, 1991).

Classroom error correction research to date points to the overall long-term superiority of indirect feedback. In longitudinal studies by Lalande (1982), Frantzen (1995), and Ferris (2006), groups of students who received indirect feedback significantly outperformed those who received direct feedback—in fact, in all three studies, the students receiving direct feedback either made no progress at all or even regressed in some error categories. On the other hand, Robb, Ross, and Shortreed (1986), who compared one group of students receiving direct feedback with three groups who received indirect feedback at differing levels of explicitness, reported no significant differences across the four treatment groups, although all four groups showed improvement in accuracy. Still, since direct feedback is easier for students to utilize in their revisions, it could be argued that even a study that shows the indirect feedback groups as equal to the direct feedback group provides evidence for the benefits of indirect feedback.

However, in recent years, several SLA researchers have completed studies suggesting the superiority of direct feedback for students' uptake and retention of information about targeted language forms such as direct and indirect articles.[10] In all cases, the errors were marked and corrected with some kind of error code, and in some studies, students received additional information about the targeted error types, such as short metalinguistic explanations of rules appended to their texts or in-class oral presentations of the rules. As I have suggested elsewhere (Ferris, 2010), the differences in approach and results between these two bodies of research may reflect distinct starting points. In the SLA studies, researchers were tracing ways in which corrective feedback could impact student writers' acquisition of specific language structures over time. In the classroom-based L2 writing studies, researchers were most interested in how feedback could facilitate not only students' immediate growth in written accuracy but also their development of transferable self-editing strategies that could help them in future writing tasks. For the former objective (written accuracy), clear, narrow, and explicit feedback might help students to master the structure in question. For the latter (self-editing strategies), a process of "guided learning and problem-solving" (Lalande, 1982, p. 140) may better serve the long-term objective of fostering student autonomy in monitoring their own writing.

The study by Ferris (2006) is unique in that it looked at the effects of different feedback treatments both in the short term (from one draft of a paper to the next) and in the long run (from the beginning to the end of the semester). Not surprisingly, it was found that in the short term, direct feedback led to more correct revisions (88 percent) than indirect feedback (77 percent). However, over the course of the semester, students who received primarily indirect feedback reduced their error frequency ratios substantially more than the students who received mostly direct feedback. Again, because direct feedback is easier for students to act on and requires less knowledge and effort on their part, it is not surprising that from one draft of a paper to the next it would show more positive effects than indirect correction. Nonetheless, as in Lalande's and Frantzen's studies, the cumulative effect of the differing treatments appeared to be that students who received indirect feedback improved in overall accuracy more than those who did not. It is also interesting to observe that in studies where student writers were asked about the type of error feedback they felt would be most helpful, more students chose indirect feedback (Ferris, 2006; Ferris & Roberts, 2001; Leki, 1991).

Explicitness of Feedback

If indirect feedback is the superior choice in at least some cases, a follow-up question is how explicit such feedback needs to be. Several studies have examined the effects of *coded* feedback (in which the type of error, such as "verb tense" or "spelling" is indicated) versus *uncoded* feedback (in which the instructor circles or underlines an error but leaves it to the student writer to diagnose and solve the problem). Though survey research indicates that students and instructors feel that more explicit (i.e., coded or labeled) feedback is preferable and even necessary (Ferris 2006; Ferris & Roberts, 2001), the text-analytic evidence that exists on this question does not support their intuitions. As previously noted, Robb, Ross, and Shortreed's (1986) study showed that there were no significant differences in student accuracy across three different indirect feedback types (coded, underlined, and checkmarks in the margins). Ferris (2006) reported that students who received uncoded indirect feedback were nearly as successful (75 percent) at self-correcting errors in revision as those who received coded indirect feedback (77 percent). In a follow-up experimental study,[11] Ferris and Roberts (2001) again found no significant differences in revision success rates between code and no-code treatment groups. Robb, Ross, and Shortreed concluded from their data that for busy writing instructors, "less time-consuming methods of directing student attention to surface errors may suffice" (1986, p. 91). On the other hand, Ferris and Roberts (2001) argued that "though the results of this study . . . suggest that a less explicit marking technique may be equally effective in the short-run, this strategy may not give adequate input to produce the reflection and cognitive engagement that helps students to acquire linguistic structures and reduce errors over time" (p. 177).[12] They suggested that if a clear and consistent system of coded feedback is paired with in-class mini-lessons that highlight the specific errors being marked, students may show more progress in the long run than if errors are simply underlined. However, at this point in time, there is no evidence to support this speculation.

Effects of Error Feedback across Different Linguistic Categories

Some researchers have also contrasted the effects of error feedback on student writing across different linguistic categories (lexical, morphological, syntactic). It has been argued that these categories represent completely different domains of linguistic knowledge and that they therefore should not be treated interchangeably by teachers and researchers (Ferris, 1999a; Truscott, 1996). Indeed, in studies that have examined and contrasted the effects of feedback on specific linguistic features, consistent differences have been found in student progress across the various error categories.[13] For instance, in the Ferris (2006) study, students made substantial progress over the course of a semester in reducing errors in verb tense and form, slight progress in reducing lexical- and noun-ending errors, and regressed (i.e., got worse) in the sentence structure and article errors categories.

Global and Local Errors

Two relevant distinctions that have been made in the literature are between "global and local" errors and between "treatable and untreatable" errors. The first distinction was introduced by Burt and Kiparsky (1972) to refer to errors that interfere with the comprehensibility of a text (*global* errors) versus more minor errors that do not impede understanding (*local* errors). This dichotomy has been progressively redefined in the subsequent error correction literature (Bates, Lane, & Lange, 1993; Hendrickson, 1978), but while it is intuitively appealing, it can be hard to operationalize for research or pedagogical purposes. For instance, Hendrickson (1978) included some of the same categories as examples of both local and global errors. It seems that the relative seriousness of particular linguistic errors may be context-dependent. Further, there is no research evidence to suggest that treating global or local errors differently makes any impact on student writing.[14]

Treatable and Untreatable Errors

In my response to Truscott's 1996 essay (Ferris, 1999a), I introduced the (at the time) ad hoc dichotomy between "treatable" and "untreatable" errors as a pedagogical distinction. A *treatable* error is related to a linguistic structure that occurs in a rule-governed way. It is treatable because the student writer can be pointed to a grammar book or set or rules to resolve the problem. An *untreatable* error, on the other hand, is idiosyncratic, and the student will need to utilize acquired knowledge of the language to self-correct it. Examples of treatable errors include verb tense and form; subject-verb agreement; article usage; plural and possessive noun endings; sentence fragments; run-ons and comma splices; some errors in word form; and some errors in punctuation, capitalization, and spelling. Untreatable errors include most word choice errors, with the possible exception of some pronoun and preposition usage, and unidiomatic sentence structure (e.g., problems with word order or with missing or unnecessary words).

Two subsequent studies have operationalized and examined the "treatable/untreatable" dichotomy. In the first (Ferris, 2006), teachers were far more likely to give indirect feedback in the case of treatable error types and direct feedback when the error fell into one of the untreatable categories, even though they had agreed at the outset of the study to give coded indirect feedback to all errors that they marked. Remarking on this finding, Chaney (1999) speculated that teachers were operating on an intuitive sense that certain errors were more amenable to self-correction than others. Because of the idiosyncratic nature of untreatable errors, it has been suggested that they are perhaps better addressed with direct feedback (Chaney, 1999; Ferris, 1999a; Hendrickson, 1980).

However, in the second study (Ferris & Roberts, 2001), which was a controlled experimental study in which all students received either indirect feedback or none at all, we found a more complex picture. While students were more successful at self-editing errors in three treatable categories (verbs, noun endings, and articles) than the two untreatable categories (word choice and sentence structure), further statistical analysis showed that the differences lay in the sentence structure category, not the word choice category. In fact, the differences in revision success rates between treatable errors and untreatable word choice errors were not significant. And while all students were less successful in correcting sentence structure errors—significantly so—they were still able, as a group, to correct them in 47 percent of the cases, compared with a range of 53–60 percent for the other four categories. This suggests that indirect feedback may be useful at least some of the time even in so-called untreatable error categories. It is worth noting that many of the student writers in those two studies were "ear learners" (primarily Generation 1.5 students), so they may simply have self-edited underlined text portions according to their own intuitions about the language (see Chapter 1; Ferris, 1999a, 2009). Again, the nature and effects of error feedback may vary dramatically according to student characteristics and other contextual variables.

Beyond Corrective Feedback: Effects of Other Classroom Interventions on Students' Written Accuracy

Giving students written feedback on their errors is not, of course, the only mechanism writing teachers have available for helping them to improve their accuracy and overall writing quality. Other techniques include teacher-student conferences and peer editing sessions, revision or rewriting after receiving feedback, in-class grammar instruction tailored to particular problematic issues in writing, and maintenance of error charts or logs so that teachers and students can track progress over time. These various options are further discussed and exemplified in Chapter 5. In this section, we will focus on evaluating the research evidence available on the efficacy of these techniques.

Alternate Forms of Error Feedback

Many writing instructors feel that one-on-one conferences with students—whether to discuss ideas, organization, or errors—are more effective than handwritten commentary or corrections (Zamel, 1985). Conferences, after all, offer immediacy and the opportunity for two-way clarification and negotiation.[15] However, there is very little research available about writing conferences with L2 students, and the published studies that do exist (Ewert, 2009; Goldstein & Conrad, 1990; Patthey-Chavez & Ferris, 1997) do not specifically examine the effects of such conferences on student errors and accuracy. Similarly, composition researchers tout the value of peer response sessions in the writing classroom (for reviews see Ferris, 2003; Ferris & Hedgcock, 2005; Liu & Hansen, 2002). Although there have been many empirical studies over the past 20 years on the nature and effects of peer feedback, none have specifically looked at the effects of peer error correction on student accuracy. Thus, though it is certainly possible that both feedback delivery systems (conferences and peer editing), together with rapidly developing technological options such as computer text analyzers or grammar checkers, may have value in helping students to edit their work and improve the accuracy and clarity of their writing, there is no empirical evidence available yet to support these assumptions.

Error Correction and Revision

Many researchers have pointed out that teacher feedback of any type is more likely to benefit student writing if it comes primarily at intermediate, rather than final, stages of the writing process—specifically, when students are allowed or even required to revise or rewrite their papers after receiving teacher feedback.[16] A number of studies already mentioned in this chapter also provide evidence that when students revised their papers after receiving error feedback, their accuracy improved, either in the short or long term.[17] On the other hand, in two studies in which one group of students revised their papers after receiving feedback while another group did not, there was no benefit as to superior accuracy for the group that revised (Frantzen, 1995; Polio, Fleck, & Leder, 1998). It is important to note that in this body of work, only one study specifically isolates revision after corrective feedback as a key variable (Chandler, 2003). In the rest, other variables in addition to revision differed across groups. For instance, in Lalande's 1982 study, his experimental group received indirect, coded feedback and revised their marked papers during in-class editing sessions, while the control group students received direct correction and did not revise their papers. Other studies vary along similar lines. In sum, while it seems likely that asking students to edit their papers after receiving error feedback not only will improve the quality of the texts under immediate consideration but will also cause writers to become more aware of and attentive to patterns of error, there is no compelling evidence as yet that the presence or absence of revision makes a difference in the long run. On the other hand, some researchers and reviewers have suggested that revision and (other forms of writing practice) is the key to long-term student improvement. This is certainly a key area for further research.

In-Class Grammar Instruction

It has also been suggested that writing teachers may need to provide in-class instruction, in the form of grammar mini-lessons and editing strategy training, to help students learn how to recognize, correct, and avoid various recurring patterns of error.[18] To my knowledge, there have been no studies to date that have looked solely at grammar instruction (separate from other variables such as feedback and revision) as a means to improve student accuracy. In several studies in which grammar instruction was intentionally combined with error feedback, students showed progress in written accuracy (Bitchener & Knoch, 2008; Ferris, 1995a; Frantzen & Rissel, 1987; Lalande, 1982; Sheen, 2007), but in other studies it did not appear to make a difference or to help students (Frantzen, 1995; Polio, Fleck, & Leder, 1998). However, the nature of the "grammar instruction" varied widely in these studies, and in some instances, it was not even described. Further, as noted by Frodesen and Holten (2003), "Even when a grammatical feature has been covered and practiced, students may not use it accurately in their own writing" (p. 142).

Most experts on the teaching of grammar to L2 students agree that classroom grammar instruction is most effective when it is carefully paired with opportunities for students to apply what they have learned to their own output. In the context of grammar and editing mini-lessons in the writing class, the most obvious applications would be for students to practice newly covered grammatical concepts by finding and correcting errors in sample student texts and then in their own texts (discussed further in Chapter 5). While it seems clear that isolated grammar instruction is unlikely to help most student writers improve, we do not yet know whether carefully planned mini-lessons that are keyed to real student writing problems and explicitly connected to other forms of intervention (such as feedback and revision exercises) will provide additional support that is needed for at least some students to improve their writing. Again, the research evidence is inconclusive because grammar instruction has not been isolated from other pedagogical techniques and because the nature of the grammar instruction itself is almost never specified in the research reports.

Error Charts

It has also been suggested that long-term progress in accuracy can be facilitated by the maintenance of error logs or charts by teachers and/or students themselves (Bates, Lane, & Lange, 1993; Ferris, 1995a, 1995c; Lalande, 1982). Error logs help students to focus on major patterns of written error and to be aware of the relative frequency of various error types as they move from one draft or assignment to the next in a writing class. Several studies to date[19] have investigated the usefulness of error logs for L2 student writers (Komura, 1999; Lalande, 1982; Roberts, 1999). In Lalande's study, the experimental group received indirect, coded feedback, did in-class revisions immediately after their marked papers were returned, and maintained error logs, outperforming the control group (as to longitudinal improvement in writing accuracy) that received direct correction and in-class grammar instruction. Lalande reports that the experimental group significantly outperformed the control group on accuracy measures at the end of the semester. However, because the two groups varied in at least four different ways (type of error feedback received, revision, in-class grammar instruction, and maintenance of error logs), it is difficult to isolate the effects of error logs. In contrast, studies completed by Komura (1999) and Roberts (1999), also described in Ferris (2006), analyzed data from groups of student writers that varied only along the error log variable. While Komura's and Roberts' studies showed no short-term benefits for error charts (i.e., revision success from one draft to the next of the same paper), a longitudinal analysis showed a clear advantage for the error log group from the beginning to the end of the semester. As noted by Roberts (1999), there were a number of technical problems with the design and implementation of the error charts. These included the use of too many error categories and codes, representing in some cases grammar terminology and rules with which the student writers were not familiar, a lack of integration of the error charts into other classroom activities, and a lack of consistency on the part of teachers and students in maintaining the charts. It is possible that if these problems had been resolved, maintenance of error charts might have shown even greater benefit for the students. However, the research database is far too small to draw any conclusions about the possible usefulness of error charts.

Student Views of Error Treatment in Writing Classes

In addition to examining empirical research evidence about the nature and effects of error feedback and other types of instructional intervention, it is important to consider student preferences and expectations. It has been assumed in the literature that L2 student writers expect and value error feedback from their teachers, and it has been claimed that the absence of such feedback could raise student anxiety, increase student frustrations, and cause students to lose confidence in their teachers (Ferris, 1999a, 2003; Ferris & Hedgcock, 2005; Frantzen, 1995; Leki, 1991). On the other hand, others have claimed that excessive attention to student errors may be offensive and demotivating to student writers and that it may be ultimately harmful to them because it deflects teacher and student time and attention away from more important aspects of writing, such as process, development of ideas, and organization (Krashen, 1984; Truscott, 1996; Zamel, 1985).

A number of studies of student opinion over the past decade or so have looked at issues surrounding feedback in general and error correction in particular. Research designs have ranged from case studies (Cohen & Cavalcanti, 1990; Ferris et al., 2010; Roberts, 1999) to large-scale surveys (e.g., Hedgcock & Lefkowitz, 1994; Montgomery & Baker, 2007; Rennie, 2000). In several cases, larger-scale questionnaire studies were combined with interviews of a smaller sample of subjects (e.g., Ferris et al., 2010; Hedgcock & Lefkowitz, 1996; Komura, 1999). This body of work can be subdivided into two larger categories: (1) studies that assess student opinions and preferences about teacher feedback in general, touching on error correction and grammar issues in conjunction with other questions; and (2) research that looks primarily at error correction in student writing, examining not only student opinions about the relative value of such feedback but specific student views about how error correction should be delivered by teachers.

In the first group of studies, student survey respondents, who were typically university ESL students in the United States (but also included foreign language subjects in the studies by Cohen, 1987, and Hedgcock & Lefkowitz, 1994, 1996) were asked about the relative merits of various types of feedback. Specifically, they were asked whether they received and/or preferred to receive feedback about content, organization, grammar, vocabulary, and mechanics. Somewhat to the dismay of the researchers in some cases, they found a strong and consistent preference for grammar feedback on the part of L2 student writers. Both Radecki and Swales (1988) and Leki (1991) noted the conflict between students' strong desire for grammar feedback and existing research evidence that suggested that error correction was not only ineffective but perhaps even harmful to the development of student writing (as later argued by Truscott, 1996). While both sets of authors suggested that writing teachers share with students the research about the limitations of error correction and the benefits of the process approach, Leki also pointed out that "it seems at best counter-productive, at worst high-handed and disrespectful of our students, to simply insist that they trust our preferences . . . . we do well at least to become aware of students' perceptions of their needs and their sense of what helps them progress" (1991, p. 210). Though Truscott (1999) anecdotally reported that his own students had adjusted well to the absence of error feedback, many teachers may find that it can be very difficult to ignore or change L2 students' views about the importance of error feedback from their writing teachers.

Later researchers, however, noted that student writers in process-oriented composition classes claimed to value feedback of all types, not just on their errors (Ferris, 1995b; Hedgcock & Lefkowitz, 1994, 1996; Montgomery & Baker, 2007). Another consistent finding across this group of studies was that instructors' priorities, as expressed through their feedback, appeared to influence students' perceptions and attitudes about the types of issues they wanted addressed through teacher feedback. In other words, if a teacher primarily gave feedback about surface-level error, that teacher's students were likely to say that they preferred to receive feedback about their errors. In general, there appeared to be a good match between what students said they wanted in teacher feedback and in the types of feedback they reported receiving from their teachers.

Finally, in this body of studies, there appeared to be little support for assertions from L1 composition researchers that student writers ignore and resent teacher feedback, especially if focused on form and errors (see, e.g., Straub, 1997). As pointed out by Leki (1990, 1991), many L2 writers have linguistic and rhetorical gaps when compared to monolingual L1 writers. Further, they may have an "overriding sense of urgency to perfect their English" paired with "less reluctance to have errors pointed out" because they do not have the same sense of stigma connected with their problems in formal written English that L1 student writers may feel (Leki, 1991, p. 205). As already noted, findings from composition studies that focus primarily on monolingual L1 writers may need to be critically re-evaluated in the light of the unique needs of L2 writers (see Chapter 1 for further discussion).

In the second group of studies on student views about feedback, students were asked specifically about the types of error feedback they found most helpful. Though different questions were asked in the various studies, some generalizations may be made. First, to the extent students complained about or had problems with teacher error correction, such problems were often connected to "implicit" suggestions (Ferris, 1995b; Radecki & Swales, 1988) such as underlining, arrows, boxes, circles, and error codes such as "vt" (verb tense) or "ro" (run-on). While students in general claimed to have little trouble understanding and utilizing teacher feedback, when they were confused, such teacher notations and shorthand were most typically the culprits. Second, students appeared to be open to a cooperative approach to error feedback in which the teacher called attention to errors through locating and labeling them but then left it to the student to attempt to make the correction in a rewrite or revision. It seemed clear from a number of disparate studies that students recognized that they were likely to learn more and become more independent as writers and editors if they had some investment in the process, rather than simply copying or noting direct corrections the teachers had made.

Third, students were uniformly hostile to error correction approaches in which the teacher did not mark errors at all but left it to the writer to find, diagnose, and solve problems by themselves. For instance, in studies by Leki (1991), Ferris and Roberts (2001), and Rennie (2000), when students were asked if they preferred teachers not to mark errors at all, no students chose this option in the first two studies, and only two students (0.6 percent) of Rennie's subjects said they would like this scenario. However, there was more variety in student responses as to whether error correction should be comprehensive (covering all errors found) or selective (focusing on the most frequent and serious errors). While the majority of students in these studies claimed to favor comprehensive correction, there was a noticeable minority that appeared to see merit in selective correction, as long as it dealt with the "most serious" errors.

Two other issues were addressed in a couple of the survey studies. As previously mentioned, when students were asked whether they preferred errors to be labeled or just located, they strongly favored errors to be labeled by type (Ferris, 2006; Ferris & Roberts, 2001; Hedgcock & Lefkowitz, 1994, 1996; Rennie, 2000). However, as already discussed, there is to date no evidence that this more precise labeling of errors makes a difference in students' short- or long-term progress in accuracy (Ferris, 2006; Ferris & Roberts, 2001; Robb, Ross, & Shortreed,1986). The other question was about the teacher's use of a red pen to mark errors, a technique that has been discouraged by L1 and L2 composition experts as being too negative and intimidating to students (seen as the teacher "bleeding all over" the student's paper). Two studies (Hedgcock & Lefkowitz, 1994, 1996; Leki, 1991) investigated this question in student surveys. In neither case did they find that their L2 subjects had strongly negative feelings about the color of ink the teacher used to mark errors. The color of ink may be even less relevant in an era of electronic feedback tools in Word documents such as Track Changes, Comments, and so forth.

What is notable about this body of student opinion studies is how consistent the findings are, despite variations in methodology and in subject characteristics. To summarize these two related lines of research, studies of student opinion about teacher feedback have consistently found the following:

- Students feel that teacher feedback on grammar and errors is extremely important to their progress as writers.
- Students in the most recent studies also see value in other types of teacher feedback (on ideas and organization).
- Student writers mostly favor comprehensive teacher marking of errors.
- Student writers, when given a choice of teacher marking strategies, tend to prefer for teachers to mark errors and give them strategies for correcting them over either direct correction of errors or less explicit indirect methods.
- Students sometimes found teachers' marking systems confusing or cumbersome.

In short, student views about error feedback appear to be reasonable, based on experience, and focused on what is best for their learning, not simply what is the least work for them or might earn them the highest grades. Teachers should carefully listen to their students' perceptions and preferences as they consider how to design their own feedback and error treatment strategies.

Possible Directions for Further Research

A review of research such as the one in this chapter often seems to raise more questions than it answers. By looking critically at an existing body of studies, we become aware (often painfully so) of the gaps in the empirical evidence on a particular topic and of the inadequacies of some of the previous lines of research. Some possible research issues that arise from the foregoing review are discussed briefly in this final section. These are relevant both to the task of evaluating previous research and planning future studies.

Methodology

One vitally important issue to examine is research methodology. For instance, the various studies on the effects of error correction methods have typically looked at extremely diverse student populations, ranging from U.S. college students taking foreign language classes (sometimes as majors, sometimes not) at U.S. universities to immigrant ESL writers who have learned English primarily through acquisition and exposure to the language rather than through formal training. Not only do subject characteristics differ on about every parameter imaginable, but their motivation and purposes for studying the language and developing their L2 writing skills are likely to be very different as well (Ferris, 1999b; Hedgcock & Lefkowitz, 1994; Reid, 1998a). Yet in many reviews of research, studies that include subjects of widely varying characteristics are treated as though they had looked at identical populations. Similar concerns can be raised about other design issues, including the characteristics of the error feedback and who was providing it, the types of student writing being considered, the types of linguistic issues covered, and methodological points such as inclusion of control groups, baseline pre-treatment data, and reporting of inter-rater reliabilities. While it is hardly controversial to point out that such issues need to be considered both in designing primary research and evaluating and reviewing secondary research, it is important to mention here because many researchers fail to control for or even consider these questions. Future research studies, and further reviews of research need to examine design and methodology issues with far more care than has been demonstrated to this point (for further discussion of this point see also Ferris, 2003, Chapter 3; 2004; 2010).

Questions for Further Research

Longitudinal AND Contextualized?

In the first edition of this book, I wrote at this point: "Most crucially, there need to be longitudinal, contextualized studies that examine the effects of error correction on students' language control, written accuracy, and writing quality" (Ferris, 2002, p. 35). Since then, there has been a great deal of research activity around the topic of written corrective feedback for L2 writers. Most of these studies (but not all) have followed the SLA research paradigm described previously, and if one considers the inclusion of a delayed post-test as evidence that a study is indeed "longitudinal," then at least some of the points in my previous statement have been more adequately addressed by researchers since 2002. However, while these studies are cleanly designed and well focused and while they incorporate control groups of students receiving no feedback, it is not possible, regardless of definition, for these studies to be considered "contextualized," as the student texts are produced under timed, experimental conditions; no revision is required or allowed; and feedback is given by researchers rather than by classroom instructors. This is not to say that these studies have not been valuable in providing additional evidence that carefully constructed error feedback can indeed benefit the writing of L2 students. However, there is still a need for more "longitudinal, contextualized" research on the effects of corrective feedback for L2 writers. In a recent article, I outlined an approach to future research that could combine the methodology of the SLA studies with that of classroom-based L2 writing studies of revision after feedback (see Ferris, 2010, Figure 1, p. 195).

In such longitudinal, contextualized research, the writing of students who receive consistent, thoughtful, and accurate error feedback needs to be compared with the writing of students who receive other forms of writing instruction but no error correction. It should be frankly noted—again—that it can be very difficult to conduct such studies, since both teachers and students have such strong biases as to the necessity for error correction that teachers would feel remiss if they did not provide it—and, perhaps more to the point, would fear hostility from their students (Truscott, 1996, 1999). Nonetheless, a compelling case for or against error correction in L2 writing classes cannot possibly be made without a substantial body of research studies along these lines.

Effective versus Ineffective Error Treatment

Inextricable from the critical question "Does error correction help students to improve their writing?" is the question of what makes error feedback effective or ineffective. As I have noted elsewhere (Ferris, 1999a), few would argue that poorly conceived, inconsistent, or inaccurate error correction is unlikely to help student writers and may well be harmful to their development. Though the answers to this question bear much more scrutiny, we at least have some starting points from the available research: (1) indirect feedback is in many cases more beneficial than direct feedback; (2) a wide range of error types, including those previously deemed "untreatable," appear to be responsive to indirect feedback; and (3) coded, labeled feedback may not be necessary in some cases. While more research should be conducted to examine all three of these generalizations with a range of student populations and in a variety of contexts, it may be most helpful from this point to examine feedback in conjunction with other types of error treatment discussed in this review—revision, grammar instruction, and the use of error charts. It would also be informative to look at whether students who are at relatively low levels of L2 proficiency benefit from different types of feedback (e.g., direct correction followed by rewriting) and error treatment than those who are more advanced.

Student Views and Individual Differences

A final direction for further research on error treatment arises from the body of work on student views of teacher feedback. It has been suggested that student writers be offered a range of feedback options by their teachers and that feedback be individually tailored to their preferences. Appealing as this suggestion may be from a humanistic, affective perspective, it certainly sounds challenging and cumbersome for teachers, and there is no empirical evidence to suggest that such accommodations make a difference, compared with the teacher simply providing feedback in way(s) she or he deems best. However, other lines of research on error correction and SLA do indicate that there is a great deal of individual variation in students' ability to process teacher feedback and utilize it for their development as writers. Such variation may come from the nature of the students' L1s, their prior exposure to the L2 and to composition instruction, motivation, personality, and learning style. The sources and implications of individual student variation in response to error treatment have not begun to receive serious investigation or attention (see also Ferris, 2006, 2010; Ferris et al., 2010). Perhaps these two lines of inquiry—stated student preferences and individual differences—can help teachers to understand better why some students make substantial progress while others make less (or none at all) in response to feedback and that they need to adjust or even tailor error treatment strategies accordingly.

Concluding Thoughts

This chapter has covered a great deal of ground in reviewing the issues surrounding error treatment for L2 writers and the research that thus far has been completed to investigate these questions. To summarize these strands of evidence, the following statements are offered:

1. Though researchers have suggested that teachers are inconsistent and inaccurate in providing error feedback to L2 student writers, there is no direct evidence to support this charge, and a couple of studies that show teachers to be fairly thorough and mostly accurate in their error feedback.

2. Scholars have also suggested that L2 writers do not attend to teachers' error feedback, but the existing evidence refutes this assertion.

3. When L2 writers revise their texts after receiving corrective feedback, those texts improve in accuracy, especially when compared with texts of students who received no feedback.

4. When students write new texts after receiving error feedback, there is mounting evidence that they demonstrate improvement in control of specific structures targeted in feedback and/or in overall accuracy of their texts.

5. Most researchers now believe that focused error feedback is superior to unfocused feedback, but there may be specific situations in which unfocused, comprehensive error feedback on a student text may be valuable.

6. Studies on the benefits of direct versus indirect error feedback report conflicting findings, and those differences may be rooted in differing research goals or starting points for the studies.

7. Though teachers and students believe that more explicit (labeled or coded) indirect error feedback is more beneficial to them than less explicit (underlined or circled but not labeled) feedback, there is no evidence thus far to support this intuition.

8. Other types of error feedback (teacher-student conferences, peer feedback, etc.) may be useful to L2 student writers, but there is no research that directly examines the benefits of such feedback or (especially) isolates the particular issue of *error* feedback as opposed to more general feedback on a range of concerns.

9. Beyond error feedback, other types of classroom interventions such as grammar instruction, required revision, or maintaining error charts may be useful, but except for a few studies that touch on these approaches in passing, there is little evidence for or against their utility.

10. Students strongly believe in the value of error feedback (and feedback on other writing issues) and have specific opinions as to which error feedback strategies are most helpful to them. In particular, when given choices, they tend to favor indirect, explicit (coded/labeled) feedback over other types.

11. Future research on error treatment should carefully consider a range of methodological issues, privilege designs that are both *longitudinal and contextualized,* and give more attention to classroom interventions that could support expert corrective feedback. Further, research should examine the effects of individual student differences on ability to benefit from error treatment approaches.

It is encouraging to observe that since the publication of the first edition of this book, our knowledge about this controversial yet important pedagogical topic has increased substantially. In answer to the big question of whether error feedback helps student writers at all, there is much more affirmative evidence from a wider range of sources. Indeed, for some researchers, it is time to move on—from the question of *if* we should provide error feedback to *how best* to do so (see, e.g., Evans et al., 2010). That *how best* question is the focus of the remainder of this book.

Questions for Discussion and Application

1. Think of your own experiences as a student writer (in any language) and/or as a teacher of writing. The first two points discussed in this chapter are (a) whether teachers do a thorough and accurate job of responding to student errors and (b) whether students in fact pay attention to teachers' error feedback. From your own experiences and observations, what are your opinions about these two points?

2. Imagine that you are teaching a writing class and a researcher comes and asks if your class could be the "controls" for his study, meaning that students would receive no error feedback on their papers during your entire course while other groups of students received different types of feedback treatments. Considering the ideas discussed in this chapter, would you agree to this plan? Why or why not? (Assume for the sake of argument that you have the authority to make this decision and that no administrator would stand in your way.)

3. Obtain two sample L2 student papers written to the same task. For the first, go through and mark any and all errors you notice. (Mark them using any method that makes sense to you.) For the second paper, read through the paper without making any marks, and identify three or four patterns of error, such as articles, verb tense, word choice, etc. Go through the paper again, and mark only those identified patterns of error. Which marking approach seemed harder to you? Which one do you think would be more beneficial to students? Why?

4. Again using two sample student papers, mark errors on the first using *direct* feedback (make the corrections yourself). On the second, provide *indirect* feedback (mark the errors but don't correct them). For the indirect feedback, you can choose whether to simply underline errors or to label/code them. Which approach seemed harder to you? Why?

5. Do you think student preferences and/or individual differences should factor into your approach to providing error feedback to student writers? Why or why not? If yes, in what way(s)?

6. Examine the final section of this chapter where directions for future research are suggested. Considering the ideas raised in this chapter and/or your own experiences and interests, brainstorm a possible research question you would pursue if you were going to design a study on error treatment for L2 writers. Also discuss approaches you might use to collect and analyze your data.

7. Obtain and read one of the primary research studies cited in this chapter. Critically evaluate it in the light of the "methodology" issues raised in the final section, the other issues raised in the chapter, and your own observations and experiences. Would you say this study provides good insights about error feedback/treatment for L2 writers? Why or why not?

Further Reading

These sources will help you go further in understanding the major themes developed in this chapter. Complete bibliographic information is provided in the References section at the end of the book. The list is presented alphabetically rather than chronologically or thematically.

Chandler, J. (2003).

Cohen, A.D., & Robbins, M. (1976).

Ellis, R., Sheen, Y., Murakami, M., & Takashima, H. (2008).

Evans, N.W., Hartshorn, K.J., McCollom, R.M., & Wolfersberger, M. (2010).

Ferris, D.R. (2006).

Ferris, D.R. (2010).

Ferris, D.R., & Roberts, B.J. (2001).

Hendrickson, J.M. (1980).

Lalande, J.F. II (1982).

van Beuningan et al. (in press).

CHAPTER 2 NOTES

1. Researchers claiming that teacher error feedback is inadequate include Cohen & Cavalcanti, 1990; Cohen & Robbins, 1976; Truscott, 1996; Zamel, 1985.

2. To be clear, researchers did not make statements in these studies such as "All teacher feedback is accurate and consistent" or "All teachers respond in the same ways." The important point, however, is that there was no mention in the research reports of independent analyses of the errors and of the teacher feedback to assess whether the corrections are of high/equivalent quality.

3. In Haswell's minimal marking method, students received checkmarks in the margins by lines of text where errors were noticed by the teacher. They were required to attempt corrections in class and were graded on their diligence in doing so.

4. In this later study, the corrections were provided by the researchers. However, the second author (Roberts) was the instructor of two of the classes studied.

5. These corrections were not always successful, as discussed in a later section. However, the point here is that the students at least attempted to address most of the teacher feedback.

6. This body of work is growing rapidly, but it includes Bitchener, Young, & Cameron (2005); Bitchener & Knoch (2010a, 2010b); Ellis et al., 2008; Sheen, 2007; and van Beuningan et al., in press.

7. The terms *direct* and *indirect* will be defined more precisely later in this chapter; readers are directed to Lalande's study for more specific details about his design. It is simply mentioned here as an example of a longitudinal study of correction that did not include a no-feedback control group.

8. Other studies that assessed longitudinal progress in accuracy in L2 writing include Kepner (1991); Polio, Fleck, & Leder (1998); Robb, Ross, & Shortreed (1986); Semke (1984); and Sheppard (1992).

9. I first came across these terms in articles by Hendrickson (1978, 1980) and have seen them frequently in subsequent decades.

10. Studies suggesting positive effects for direct feedback include Bitchener & Knoch (2008); Ellis et al. (2008); and Sheen (2007).

11. Though Ferris and Roberts's (2001) study was published earlier, the data in Ferris (2006) were actually collected first, and the Ferris/Roberts study was specifically designed to further investigate questions that had arisen during the first study.

12. Also, the majority of the student participants in Ferris (2006) and Ferris and Roberts (2001) were resident immigrants rather than newer arrivals, and it has been suggested (see Ferris, 1999b; Ferris et al., 2010; and Ch. 1) that

such students tend to use acquired intuitions rather than formally learned rules to self-edit their texts. A similar study completed with an international or EFL population might yield different results.

13. Studies of error feedback focused on specific linguistic categories include Ferris, 1995a, 2006; Ferris & Roberts, 2001; Frantzen, 1995; Frantzen & Rissel, 1987; Lalande, 1982; and Sheppard, 1992.

14. This is not to say that varying one's approach for different types of error might not be an effective pedagogical strategy. For example, if a student's lexical choices or sentence structure problems render portions of his or her text incomprehensible, the teacher's best (or even only) choice might be to conference one-on-one with the writer or to reformulate that portion of the text (if possible). However, a relatively small morphological error such as a dropped plural or past-tense endings could addressed fairly efficiently and effectively through direct or indirect feedback at the point of error.

15. See Ferris (2008) and Ferris & Hedgcock (2005) for specific suggestions about conducting effective error conferences.

16. Sources on the topic of revision after correction include Ferris, 1995b, 1997; James, 1998; Krashen, 1984; Zamel, 1985.

17. Studies demonstrating improvement in student revisions after corrective feedback include Ashwell, 2000; Chandler, 2003; Fathman & Whalley, 1990; Ferris, 1995a, 1997, 2006; Ferris & Roberts, 2001; Frantzen & Rissel, 1987; Lalande, 1982; and Truscott & Hsu, 2008.

18. Sources supportive of supplemental grammar instruction include Bates, Lane, & Lange, 1993; Byrd & Reid, 1998; Ferris, 1995c, 2003; Ferris & Hedgcock, 2005; Frodesen, 1991; and Frodesen & Holten, 2003.

19. The studies by Komura (1999) and Roberts (1999) were both M.A. theses that grew out of data from the larger study published as Ferris (2006).

Chapter 3

Preparing Teachers of L2 Writers to Treat Student Error

For many writing instructors, the prospect of responding to students' errors (Chapter 4), providing strategy training and grammar instruction (Chapter 5), or proactively developing students' academic language (Chapter 6) may appear rather daunting. Not only does the teacher need to sort through a range of pedagogical options, materials, and techniques, but effective treatment of error also requires that instructors themselves have solid linguistic knowledge and analysis skills. In this chapter, we discuss *what* teachers of L2 writers[1] need to know about grammar and language instruction (including corrective feedback) and *how* they can acquire such knowledge and build their skills.

Understanding the Problem

Teachers' Error Treatment Strategies May Not Always Be Effective

It is important to acknowledge that unless writing teachers specifically make the effort to prepare themselves to deal with student errors, they may do so less effectively than they should. In Truscott's (1996) critique of grammar correction in the L2 writing class, he discusses teachers' lack of knowledge and preparation under the rubric of "practical problems" that impede even the potential effectiveness of error feedback:

> First, the teacher must realize that a mistake has been made. The well-known problems involved in proof-reading show that this step cannot be taken for granted . . . . If teachers do recognize an error, they still may not have a good understanding of the correct use—questions regarding grammar can be very difficult, even for experts, and someone who writes or speaks English well does not necessarily understand the principles involved . . . . Thus, teachers may well know that an error has occurred but not know exactly why it is an error. If they do understand it well, they might be unable to give a good explanation; problems that need explaining are often very complex. (pp. 350–351)

To Truscott's description could be added the observation by Williams (1981) that readers do not always notice errors unless they are specifically looking for them (and sometimes not even then). Further, Truscott's quotation implies that some writing instructors may not be adequately prepared in formal grammar and pedagogy to address the challenging task of providing effective error feedback and supplemental grammar instruction. What could further be added is that, even among prospective or practicing writing instructors, there are varying degrees of competence and control over formal grammar and mechanics in teachers' own language usage. In short, teachers of L2 writers may need to build their own formal knowledge of the structure of the target language before they can successfully impart this information through error feedback or classroom instruction to their students.

Several of the studies discussed in Chapter 2 provided counterevidence to Truscott's assertions about the dismal state of teachers' error feedback. However, on further examination, we can make an important observation: The teachers who provided the feedback in those studies were well trained and/or experienced in working with L2 writers' errors. For instance, in Ferris (2006), two of the instructors had M.A. degrees in

TESOL from the same university, a program that emphasized preparation in teaching academic writing and in pedagogical grammar; the third had been teaching ESL writing classes in that program for some 20 years and had been elevated to a supervisor position for that course. It may well be the case that they are not entirely representative of other teachers of L2 writers in different contexts.[2]

Two more recent studies of teachers' response practices lend support to the speculation that among writing teachers there is a range of abilities and approaches specifically with regard to the treatment of error. Lunsford and Lunsford (2008) collected samples of teacher feedback from all over the United States and examined 877 student papers marked by their teachers. They found that teachers marked about 40 percent of the errors independently counted by the researchers and that there were disparities between the errors most frequently *made* by the student writers and those *marked* by the teachers. The types of errors marked also varied widely across the sample of teachers. This study suggests that when teachers' marking strategies are simply observed and described (rather than being manipulated in some way for a research project), there is a great deal of variation from teacher to teacher.

In another recent study (Ferris et al., 2011; Ferris, Liu, & Rabie, 2011), 129 college-level writing instructors were surveyed and some were interviewed about a range of response practices, including their approaches to error treatment. While all of the instructors surveyed said they provided language-focused feedback at least some of the time, respondents described a system of mostly direct correction with error codes, and only 15 percent said that they ever used indirect correction techniques. Nor were the error feedback techniques observed always exemplary. In one interview, for example, a teacher said that he marked "patterns" of student errors, but when samples of his error feedback were analyzed, this pattern-marking consisted of him painstakingly typing "[comma]" anywhere a comma was missing. While a student writer likely could go back and insert the missing commas based on those cues, there was no attempt to explain to the student what the rule or problem was or how the error could be avoided in the future. Neither of these two studies was explicitly designed to assess the effectiveness of teachers' corrective feedback, but they paint a more complicated picture of what classroom teachers actually do in responding to their students' texts—and the picture provides some support for Truscott's rather dismal assessment quoted earlier (see page 58).

Teacher Preparation Programs May Not Adequately Address Error Treatment

As discussed in Chapter 1, the term *L2 writer* has become more complex and requires careful definition. As a result, in many contexts, both in the United States and elsewhere, monolingual L1 writers and multilingual L2 writers may be learning side-by-side in the same writing courses. This means that these L2 writers may be taught by instructors who have composition training, ESL training, a combination of both—or neither. For instance, in the study by Ferris, Liu, and Rabie (2011; see also Ferris et al., 2011), some writing instructors had PhDs in literature, others had graduate degrees in creative writing, some had TESOL training, and some had rhetoric/composition training. To work effectively with L2 writers, instructors should have preparation in and knowledge about these concepts (see also CCCC, 2009; Ferris, 2009):

- second language and literacy acquisition processes
- the linguistic structure/grammar of the target language
- principles and theories of composition instruction
- the ways that writing in an L2 can differ from writing in an L1
- principles and (best) practices of pedagogical grammar, especially grammar in the writing course
- principles for providing effective response (of all types) to a diverse population of student writers.

In practice, however, many instructors receive pre-service training in composition but none in linguistics, grammar, or L2 acquisition, while others obtain preparation in language teaching but little in composition or writing (and in many TESOL programs, courses on teaching writing are optional). Though teachers can and do learn a great deal from classroom experience, both the recent studies just described and years of observation lead me to believe that error treatment for L2 writers in real-world classrooms ranges from excessive to haphazard to ineffective to nonexistent. The various teacher preparation paths surely account for much of the disparity across different writing classes.

Teachers May Have Philosophical Objections to Error Treatment

This problem is related to the previous one. As noted in Chapter 1, composition theorists have for decades ignored, minimized, or even openly disparaged any issues related to error treatment in writing courses. This philosophical stance was taken up and is still held today by at least some L2 specialists (e.g., Krashen, 1984; Truscott, 1996, 2007; Zamel, 1985). Though there is no evidence whatsoever that this hard-line view has ever been accepted by classroom instructors, let alone their students, it likely has affected teacher-preparation programs in various contexts. Instructors completing those programs may find themselves in the awkward position of believing that they should be morally opposed to addressing errors in student writing but confronting the very real language gaps of their students (including even monolingual L1 writers)—yet without any practical preparation as to how to address those gaps through their feedback and instruction.[3]

To summarize this discussion, Truscott (1996) is probably correct that many classroom instructors of L2 writers do not provide adequate and effective error feedback to their students. However, it is important to observe that the situation is not quite as hopeless as it may sound. Teacher preparation programs in composition and language teaching can be revamped to provide more adequate practical training for future teachers of diverse student populations, and current instructors can gather information and resources and learn (or improve) their skills. Applying the following principles will help to better prepare writing instructors for the challenging yet crucial task of error treatment for L2 writers.

Preparing Teachers for Error Treatment: Five Principles

1. Teachers of L2 writers need to study aspects of grammar that are particularly problematic for non-native speakers of English.

Studies of errors made by student writers who are monolingual native speakers of English have highlighted issues such as punctuation of sentences and clauses, pronoun reference, modification problems, and lexical errors (Connors & Lunsford, 1988; Lunsford & Lunsford, 2008). While L2 writers may also have trouble with commas, apostrophes, semi-colons, pronouns, and lexical choice, their more serious and frequent issues are related to language structures that are almost never problematic for monolingual English native speakers. These include verb tense and aspect issues, the use of articles and other determiners, noun endings (plural and possessive inflectional endings), errors in word form (such as using a noun form where an adjective is contextually required), and word order. To be able to recognize such errors in written discourse and to address them in talking to students, prospective teachers of L2 writers need to acquire substantial knowledge of these issues:

- the forms, meanings, and uses of the different verb tense and aspect combinations in English
- the forms, meanings, and uses of active and passive voice constructions

- the basic verb types (transitive, intransitive, and linking) and the constraints on each type as to passivization, addition of direct objects, etc.
- the auxiliary forms that can be added to verb phrases and the effects of auxiliaries on the use of inflectional morphemes (i.e., tense/aspect markers) in the verb phrase
- the basic types of nouns (abstract, concrete, collective, count, non-count), and the implications of these types for article usage and inflectional endings
- the general rules governing subject-verb agreement
- the differences in meaning and use between definite and indefinite articles
- basic clause and sentence patterns and how they should be combined and punctuated
- differences in form and function among nouns, verbs, adjectives, and adverbs and how to select the correct form when constructing a sentence.

While this list will certainly not cover all of the possible problems that L2 learners may encounter with English grammar, it addresses the most frequent and serious issues typically found in L2 student writing (see Chapter 4, especially Table 4.1, for further discussion of common L2 errors).

Teachers of L2 writers (present or future) should examine the bulleted list (on page 62 and above) and assess themselves honestly: Could they clearly, accurately, and concisely define the terms? Could they provide examples of the structure that are useful and unambiguous? Could they identify patterns of these types of errors in actual student writing? Perhaps the even more painful question to ask is, do they consistently control those structures in their own writing? In any place where the answer to that self-assessment is no, writing instructors should commit themselves to a program of learning more about the target language so that they in turn can analyze student writing and provide their own students with tools and strategies that will help them improve. To put it bluntly, we cannot teach what we have not mastered ourselves.[4]

Current or prospective teachers who are unable to take a course that specifically prepares them to deal with these linguistic issues may wish to acquire a reference library that explains these various constructions either for teachers or for students themselves. It is helpful to have available both one or more teacher reference grammar books and several ESL grammar/editing textbooks, the former for the depth of explanation and illustrations that teachers need to be well prepared, and the latter to give instructors a sense of how much information to present to students.[5]

2. Teachers of L2 writers need practice in recognizing and identifying errors in student writing.

A novice teacher of L2 writing may easily become overwhelmed by the language problems in students' texts, especially if the students are at fairly low levels of second language proficiency. It is worth the time and effort to work with more experienced writing teachers or teacher educators to practice identifying, classifying, and correcting errors in a set of student papers. This can happen either formally, in a class on teaching grammar or writing or in a practicum setting, or informally, as a teacher who needs experience in this area apprentices herself or himself to a more experienced writing instructor. Several examples of possible practice exercises to help teachers develop or improve their skills in identifying error types and patterns in student writing (which can be used for self-study, in class, or during a workshop) are provided in Appendix 3.1.

Such practice helps writing instructors not only to assess whether they are accurately and thoroughly finding and identifying errors in student writing, but it also helps build metacognitive awareness of the teacher's own preconceived ideas and biases about what constitutes "correct" writing—which may represent individual taste or pet peeves that may or may not be all that important or useful to student writers. To take one of many possible examples, imagine that you are reading a student paper and find a word or phrase that is not exactly wrong but that you think could be improved. Perhaps your rewrite is more appropriate as to formality or informality of the register; perhaps it is more idiomatic; or maybe it simply sounds better, at least to your eyes or ears. Would that construction be a target for your corrective feedback, or would you focus more intentionally on patterns of actual error, such as problems with verb tense, articles, or word order? Depending on your answer to that question, what does it say about your philosophy toward the purpose of corrective feedback on student writing? Practice activities involving analysis of student errors may help pre-service and in-service writing instructors to notice and explain (or defend) their own strategies, which in turn could lead to reflection and improvement.

3. Teachers of L2 writers need practice in developing lessons and teaching grammar points and editing strategies to their writing students.

In-class mini-lessons on language can help students to understand the rules and issues surrounding points of English grammar that are troublesome for L2 student writers (e.g., when to use simple past vs. present perfect tenses or when to use definite, indefinite, or zero articles in noun phrases, etc.). Chapter 5 presents principles for designing effective mini-lessons as well as several examples. However, it can be harder than it seems to learn to design effective mini-lessons. Teacher preparation courses and workshops can help writing instructors to develop these skills. Specifically, the subskills required to prepare mini-lessons on grammar/language include the following:

- identifying, narrowing, and sequencing target grammar/language points most useful for a specific group of student writers

- using resources (teacher reference books, grammar/ editing textbooks, websites, etc.) to construct brief, well-focused explanations of the targeted structure and to find/create clear and accessible examples for these short, deductive presentations
- finding good examples of the target language point that naturally occur in authentic texts (professional or student-authored) for discovery/analysis activities (see Chapter 5)
- creating practice exercises and editing guides that not only assess students' understanding of the target point and any rules governing its usage but also help students apply them to their own current and future writing
- creating a mini-lesson plan detailing the procedures and instructions needed to execute the mini-lesson in an allotted period of time
- finding ways to integrate and reinforce these mini-lessons as the course continues (e.g., through building points explicitly taught in-class into later rounds of peer review and teacher feedback).

Because the development of mini-lessons takes time and outside resources, helping teachers to practice and improve these subskills may best be accomplished through an out-of-class assignment sequence[6] in which aspiring teachers are led through the process of:

a. analyzing a subset of student papers from the same class (5–10 should suffice) and identifying a list of possible topics for language mini-lessons based on class needs
b. choosing one specific topic for the practice mini-lesson and researching the ways various print and online resources approach this topic
c. creating the components of the mini-lesson (discovery activity, deductive explanation, practice activity, application activity, lesson procedures)

   d. sharing or demonstrating the mini-lesson for peers and more experienced teachers and receiving feedback

   e. for syllabus design purposes, creating a list of possible mini-lesson topics for this particular class, sequencing it logically, thinking about how to reinforce earlier lessons throughout the course, and integrating the mini-lessons smoothly into other writing course activities.

Appendix 3.1 provides an example of a mini-lesson assignment used in an undergraduate teacher preparation course for future teachers of writing.

4. Teachers of L2 writers need to understand the principles of second language acquisition and of composition theory.

This chapter thus far has focused on building teachers' knowledge of specific grammatical concepts and of techniques for responding to student error and teaching grammar to student writers. However, it is also important that such teacher awareness be embedded in the big picture of second language acquisition theory—that mastery of second language forms and structures takes considerable time and may well not happen for many adult learners without effective instruction, that differences between L1 and L2 forms may lead to student errors in writing, and that individual differences in learning styles and motivation may affect students' responsiveness to grammar teaching techniques and to editing strategy training. Pre-service teachers should ideally have both introductory and advanced coursework that covers language and literacy acquisition processes and individual differences, among other issues. Practicing teachers should also be familiar with books and articles that emphasize or include the applications of SLA theory to the teaching and learning of grammar.[7]

Beyond considering the implications of SLA theory and research for the teaching of grammar, writing teachers need to keep grammar and error issues firmly in perspective. As writing theorists have reminded us, there are many issues beyond error that should concern L2 writers and their teachers. After all, the frequency of errors in a student text is not the sole or even the most important indicator of overall writing quality. Process approach advocates remind us that students learn simply from the process and practice of writing and that we should facilitate and mediate these processes and help the students avoid short-circuiting their thinking because of premature and excessive attention to forms and errors (Krashen, 1984; Sommers, 1982; Spack, 1988; Zamel, 1982, 1985). Scholars in contrastive rhetoric point out that, to the degree L2 student texts sound "wrong," they may be utilizing thinking and rhetorical patterns from their L1 traditions rather than simply making mistakes in the L2 (Connor, 1996; Connor & Kaplan, 1987; Kaplan, 1966). Experts in genre analysis suggest that rather than analyzing linguistic forms and errors in isolation, we consider the purposes for which student texts are being produced (e.g., Coxhead & Byrd, 2007; Johns, 1997, 2003, 2009; Swales, 1990; Tardy, 2009). Writing teachers therefore, as they consider the treatment of error in student writing, need to consider its relative importance in student writing processes and products and the impact of L1 knowledge and literacy experience on error. While we should not neglect attention to student accuracy and clarity in writing, we also should not give it *more* attention than it deserves. Accuracy concerns should at all times be balanced with development of students' ideas and rhetorical strategies as well as consideration of the (in)effectiveness of their own writing processes.

Thus, as previously noted, writing instructors need to think carefully about how error treatment will fit into their overall course syllabus. For instance, at what points will they provide error feedback on student writing—only on the final or penultimate draft of a revised paper? On homework or in-class writing assignments? Will they utilize peer review sessions to help students learn editing strategies? Will students be asked to analyze and reflect on their own errors and their progress? How many in-class mini-lessons will teachers deliver, and on what topics? Will the mini-lessons be given to the whole class, to smaller groups, or to individuals? What other resources (textbooks, websites, other online course materials, tutoring, workshops, etc.) are available to students outside of class as they work on language/error issues, and how will instructors evaluate and guide students toward these outside resources, as necessary and appropriate?

We will discuss these suggestions in more detail in Chapters 4–5 and again in the Postscript; we note them here simply to remind us that part of teacher preparation for error treatment involves thoughtful advance course and lesson planning, as well as effective strategies for feedback itself. One thing is certain, however: Absent such consideration and thoughtful decision-making, error treatment will not, in all likelihood, be as effective as it needs to be.

5. Teachers of L2 writers should become familiar with language structures needed for different task types and academic disciplines.

While understanding the structures and rules behind common language errors made by L2 writers is an important first step in teacher preparation, instructors should also be thinking proactively not just about *eradicating errors* in writing but also about helping their students to *develop control of academic language.* For example, rather than just giving feedback to students about errors in their verb usage, teachers could be showing students how to correctly form the passive voice, when passive voice should be avoided, and when it is appropriate and even expected (e.g., in some scientific writing). Similarly, instead of simply marking "pronoun errors," teachers could help students investigate what types of tasks might require/allow first-, second-, or third-person pronoun usage; how to avoid pronoun agreement errors such as "**a student** should not start writing **their** paper the night before it is due," and so forth. We will talk more specifically about strategies for academic language development in the writing class in Chapter 6. For now, we will note that another essential element of teacher preparation is learning about such structures—form, meaning, and usage—so that they can teach lessons and give feedback to their students about them.

Specifically, teacher preparation should include an introduction to *corpus linguistics,* a very active area of applied linguistics research. In corpus linguistics, large quantities of texts in the target language are computer-analyzed for relative frequencies of specific lexical items and morphological and syntactic constructions (e.g., Biber, 1988; Biber et al., 1999). The benefit of corpus linguistics research for writing teachers is that it systematically identifies the types of language constructions that occur or co-occur in various kinds of text types. For example, the Academic Word List (Coxhead, 2000) identifies 557 word families found in a broad range of English language academic texts across a range of disciplines; this analysis is based on a corpus of more than 3.5 million words. Writing instructors desiring to build students' general academic vocabulary can consult this resource to help them identify possible targets for analysis and instruction (see Chapter 6; see also Coxhead, 2006; Coxhead & Byrd, 2007).[8] In short, rather than simply guessing at what might be useful grammar or vocabulary to teach, writing instructors can rely on empirically rigorous research findings.

The problem with corpus research for classroom teachers is that conducting it and even reading it demands a fairly high level of sophistication in linguistics, statistics, and software/ programming applications—knowledge that only applied linguists with the interest and opportunity for specialized training can truly master (Conrad, 2005; Ferris, 2011). However, a growing list of classroom resources based on corpus research is available, with more being developed. These include how-to articles and chapters for teachers as well as classroom textbooks based on corpus research findings.[9] While learning about and applying corpus linguistics research to the teaching of writing can seem challenging, it is an important step in the preparation of writing teachers who want to be up-to-date and principled in their selection of language structures on which to focus.

Concluding Thoughts

Over the years I have worked in teacher preparation programs, I have fielded office visits, phone calls, and email inquiries that begin as follows: "In 25 words or fewer, can you tell me how to teach English as a Second Language?" or "I've just been hired to teach English abroad in (fill in name of country), and I have neither the time for nor interest in obtaining any training before I go. What materials or resources can you recommend for me?" My typical response to such questions is something like this: "There is more to teaching English (or any other language) effectively than just knowing how to speak English. If you want to do it well, you will have to undertake a program of preparation."

This advice (which nearly all of these walk-ins ignore, by the way) holds true especially for writing teachers who want to treat student error effectively. Being a fairly competent user of the English language does not in and of itself prepare teachers to diagnose and respond to student error and to explain grammatical concepts in English. I can attest to this firsthand, as can any experienced writing teacher. As an undergraduate English major, I won academic honors from my university and my department. I was an extremely proficient writer who rarely made a mistake in grammar or spelling (even before computers). But during my first year in a M.A. TESOL program, I was tutoring ESL writers in our campus writing center. I vividly remember being asked something innocuous such as, "What's the difference between a direct and indirect object?" and realizing that *I had no idea how to answer the question*! I could use the language accurately myself, and I could find errors in student writing and suggest correct forms. But I could not explain to the students why the form was wrong and how to avoid such errors the next time they wrote. My panicked response was to sign up for an English grammar class (which was not even required for M.A. TESOL students at the time) the very next semester.

My own experience as a teacher and as a teacher educator convinces me that teachers of L2 writers *can and should* learn to treat student errors effectively. In-service teachers who are beyond their own teacher preparation programs may need to do some reading, to audit a grammar class, to attend workshops or conference presentations on grammar teaching, or to apprentice themselves to a more experienced teacher who can mentor them in analyzing and responding to student errors and in classroom grammar instruction. Before we can prepare our students to cope with errors in their writing—not to mention real-world expectations for accurate and clear texts—we must prepare ourselves.

Questions for Discussion and Application

1. This chapter suggests—based on existing research and observation—that many writing teachers may not approach error treatment in their classes as intentionally and effectively as they should/could. Considering your own experiences as a student writer and/or a teacher, do you agree with this generalization, or is it too negative?

2. This chapter definitely argues that teachers of L2 writers need specific preparation in linguistics, grammar, language acquisition, and composition theory and pedagogy. Did you receive this kind of formal preparation (or, if you are in a teacher preparation program now, are you receiving it)? Do you agree that these are necessary? Why or why not?

3. Look at the suggestions for learning how to analyze student writing for errors and for learning how to prepare mini-lessons, together with the sample training activities in Appendix 3.1. Have you ever had this kind of practice? Do you think it would be helpful, or have you (in your opinion) gained the experience and skills you need without such practice exercises?

4. One section of the chapter talks about how to integrate various aspects of error treatment into a writing course syllabus. What are your views on the importance of these activities, relative to the other concerns of a writing course?

5. If possible, obtain an actual writing class syllabus (or two or three)—either one you've used or one written by an experienced writing instructor. Can you tell from the syllabus how error treatment is integrated? If you cannot tell, or you think the approach is inadequate, brainstorm ways you would revise the syllabus to address the issue more intentionally and/or effectively.

6. If available, read one of the suggested sources (in Further Reading or in Chapter Note 9) on the applications of corpus linguistics for the teaching of L2 writing/ writers. Do you find the approach and arguments interesting, daunting, or troubling? Could you see yourself incorporating ideas from corpus research into your own teaching of writing? If yes, how might you do so? If no, why not?

Further Reading

These sources will help you go further in understanding the major themes developed in this chapter. Complete bibliographic information is provided in the References section at the end of the book. The list is presented alphabetically rather than chronologically or thematically.

Byrd, P., & Bunting, J. (2008).
Conrad, S.M. (2005).
Conrad, S.M. (2008).
Coxhead, A. (2000).
Coxhead, A., & Byrd, P. (2007).
Ferris, D.R. (2007).
Ferris, D.R., Liu, H., & Rabie, B. (2011).
Folse, K.S. (2008).
Johns, A.M. (2009).
Lee, I. (2009).

Appendix 3.1
Sample Assignment Types for
Teacher Preparation Courses

A. Assignment in Practicum Course

Ask students to write an in-class essay during the first week of instruction. For each student text, prepare an individualized error analysis, following the procedures and examples shown in Appendix 4.1 and Figure 4.2.

B. Assignments for "Teaching ESL Writing" Course

1. *In-Class Activity.* Give students three copies of an excerpt (about 100–150 words, or 1–2 good-sized paragraphs) of an ESL student text containing a variety of error types. Tell the students to mark the text in three different ways:

- Underline, circle, or highlight all errors they find.
- Label errors using codes from a standard list.
- Provide correct forms for all errors found.

Then discuss with students the strengths, weaknesses, and challenges they discovered with each technique. An alternative approach would be to provide three different student excerpts.

2. *Out-of-Class Assignments*

- Design and administer a survey of ESL writing teachers and/or students about their preferences as to grammar instruction and error feedback.
- Design and administer a grammar knowledge pre-test that assesses the formal knowledge of a target student population.
- Consult 3–4 different grammar texts to prepare a lesson on a specific grammar point.
- Design two in-class activities for grammar/editing instruction, using a sample student text for text analysis and/or editing practice.

[Last two bullets adapted from Ferris & Hedgcock, 2005, Application Activities 7.4–7.5 pp. 293–294.]

C. Sample Questions for MA TESOL Comprehensive Examination

You have received copies of two student papers taken from an ESL 5 class at Sacramento City College. [ESL 5 is a freshman composition course designated for ESL students.]

Assume that you have a diverse class of about 25 students and that it is fairly early in the semester. The papers you have are from the first out-of-class assignment the students have completed. Complete the following steps:

(1) Complete an **error analysis** for each paper.

(2) Assume that the errors you found in the papers are generalizable to a significant number of students in the class. Based on your analysis, create **two, 50-minute lesson plans** in which you will address one or more of the problems you saw in the student papers. You may create two separate lessons on two different error/editing topics or one lesson with two connected parts. **You must use all or part of the student papers you have analyzed for at least part of your lessons.**

(3) Write a **rationale** in which you explain the results of your error analyses and how they helped you focus your lesson plans. Also explain the pedagogical choices you made in designing the lesson plans.

D. Assignment for Undergraduate English Education Course

Mini-Lesson & Presentation

Overview: You will develop a mini-lesson (10–25 minutes in length, not including any homework activities you might assign before and/or after the lesson) for a writing class. You will also sign up for mini-lesson topics on _____ (bad day to be absent!).

1. Prepare a handout packet containing the following materials:
   - A cover page that explains what topic you chose and the specific procedures you would use to teach it (like a lesson plan)
   - Materials you would use to teach the lesson (include student handouts, PowerPoint slides, teacher "script" and answer keys, etc.)
   - The mini-lesson MUST include the following required components. Not all of them must be completed in class, but you must explain on your procedures page when the students would complete them (i.e., as a warm-up in class or for homework before the mini-lesson and/or as a follow-up in class or for homework after the lesson). Required components are:

     a. **A discovery activity** in which students analyze a model (e.g., a sample introduction; a text where they could observe how semi-colons are used; etc.)

     b. **A deductive presentation** where you BRIEFLY teach about the lesson topic, including (as applicable) definitions and examples

    c. **A follow-up exercise** in which students practice what they have learned with a model (student text, literary text, etc.)

    d. **An application exercise** in which students are explicitly directed to apply what they have learned to something they have written or are in the process of writing.

Label each page of the handout with your name and with a title that clearly indicates the specific topic of the lesson (e.g., use of quotation marks; writing good titles).

2. Write a 2–3 page essay in which you explain why you chose this topic, how and why you developed your mini-lesson in the way that you did, and what you found most challenging and interesting about preparing your lesson.

3. For your in-class presentation, you will have 15 minutes to explain to your classmates what your mini-lesson covers and how you approach teaching it. Prepare an overhead(s) or PowerPoint slides (three points extra credit for using PowerPoint) that present your key speaking points in concise form. Consider this an opportunity for all of you to share your original ideas and insights with one another and to create a resource (the class set of lesson plans) that may be valuable to you in your future teaching. At the end of your presentation, take any questions, comments, or suggestions from your classmates.

CHAPTER 3 NOTES

    1. In the first edition of this book, the term *L2 writing teachers* was used frequently, especially in this particular chapter. However, recognizing that in many contexts nowadays, instructors may be working with mixed L1/L2 populations in their classes, I have changed the wording where appropriate to *teachers of L2 writers.*

    2. These two observations—that studies show that teachers can give accurate, comprehensive, and effective error feedback to student writers and that not all teachers in every context do so—are not necessarily contradictory. Rather, they suggest that while writing teachers *can* treat error effectively, they will need to be thoughtful and intentional in developing their skills for doing so.

    3. L1 composition scholars also acknowledge this philosophical/practical dilemma faced by teachers. See, e.g., Anson (2000); MacDonald (2007); and Santa (2006).

4. Experienced writing or ESL teachers likely all have at least one story to tell of blundering into and through an off-the-cuff grammar lesson that went poorly because they were unprepared to provide explanations or examples and/or to answer student questions, leading to more confusion than enlightenment!

5. For teacher reference, some possible (and accessible) titles to consider include Barry (2002); Celce-Murcia & Larsen-Freeman (1998); and Folse (2009). Editing textbooks for L2 students include Folse, Solomon, & Smith-Palinkas, 2003; and Lane & Lange, 1999. An example of an editing handbook is Raimes, 2004. See also the corpus-informed resources described in Chapter 6. Please note, however, that while all of these titles are in print at this time of writing, they may not always remain so. The list can be considered illustrative of the types of resources that could be useful for in-service writing instructors needing to build their own knowledge and skills.

6. Samples of teacher preparation activities along the lines described can be in found in Ferris and Hedgcock (2005, Application Activities, 7.4–7.5, pp. 293–294).

7. Examples of books that apply SLA research to the teaching/learning of grammar include the ones cited above in Note 5. See also Byrd & Reid (1998); Doughty & Williams (1998); and James (1998).

8. Two excellent online resources that utilize the Academic Word List (AWL) are the Compleat Lexical Tutor: www.lextutor.ca/ and the AWL Highlighter tool: www.nottingham.ac.uk/~alzsh3/acvocab/awlhighlighter.htm. URLs were current at the time of writing (retrieved 8/5/11), but readers should note that they may be subject to change.

9. Interested readers might start with Joy Reid's (2008) edited collection, *Writing Myths*, especially the chapters by Folse, Byrd & Bunting, and Conrad. A good introductory piece is Conrad (2005); see also Ferris (2011). An excellent recent article focused on teacher preparation is Coxhead & Byrd (2007), published in the *Journal of Second Language Writing*. Finally, teachers might consult two very recent books on using corpora in the language classroom by Bennett (2010) and Reppen (2010).

Chapter 4

Responding to Student Errors: Issues and Strategies

As discussed in Chapter 1, there has been some confusion and even controversy about whether teachers ought to mark student errors at all. Process advocates have argued that excessive attention to student errors may short-circuit students' writing and thinking processes, making writing only an exercise in practicing grammar and vocabulary rather than a way to discover and express meaning (Zamel, 1982, 1985). Some error correction researchers and reviewers have examined the evidence about the effects of grammar feedback on student development and concluded that it is a waste of teacher energy and deflects student attention from more important issues (e.g., Krashen, 1984; Truscott, 1996).

However, as discussed in Chapters 1 and 2, there is increasing empirical evidence to argue that *well-constructed* error feedback, especially when combined with judiciously delivered strategy training and grammar mini-lessons (see Chapters 5 and 6), is not only highly valued by students but may also be of great benefit to their development as writers and to their overall second language acquisition. This chapter, therefore, proceeds on the assumption that teacher-supplied error feedback has potential to be extremely beneficial to ESL student writers and explores various practical questions raised by the endeavor of providing such feedback:

- *Which errors* should be corrected?
- *When* should error feedback be provided?
- *How* should teachers give error feedback?

- How can teachers help students to *process and utilize* error feedback effectively?
- How can ESL writing teachers *use their time wisely* and avoid burnout in giving error feedback?

The subtopics and suggestions discussed in this chapter should be relevant both to specialized L2 writing classes and to mainstream courses that include a mix of L2 students and monolingual English speakers.

Choosing Which Errors to Mark

Comprehensive versus Selective Error Correction

Many advocates of error correction warn against attempting to mark *all* student errors because of the very real risk of exhausting teachers and overwhelming students. For example, in a large-scale study by Ferris (2006), the three ESL composition teachers, who were attempting to mark and code nearly all of the student errors in conjunction with the research project, would sometimes mark well over 100 errors on one paper 2 to 3 pages (slightly less than 800 words long)—and yet the researchers noted that the instructors did not, despite their best efforts, catch all of the students' errors! It has also been suggested that error feedback may be most effective when it focuses on *patterns* of error, allowing teachers and students to attend to, say, two or three major error types at a time, rather than dozens of disparate errors. This selective error-correction strategy helps students learn to make focused passes through their texts to find particular types of errors to which they may be most prone and to master grammatical terms and rules related to those specific errors (see Chapter 5).

However, an important counterargument in favor of comprehensive error feedback was recently made by Evans et al. (2010) and Hartshorn et al. (2010): In the real world, accuracy is valued and (near-) perfection expected. Students thus need to learn to edit their entire texts, not only two or three selected error patterns, and teachers' comprehensive error feedback can help call writers' attention to the range of problems and issues that their texts may present. Both sides of the comprehensive-versus-selective debate have merit, but the positions are not mutually exclusive. Rather, teachers need to identify their purposes for marking at any point in the writing course. For example, if their goal is to help students identify and learn to edit their most pervasive error patterns—as a valuable self-editing and learning strategy (see Chapter 5)—they may provide selective, pattern-oriented error feedback at a particular point in time. Similarly, if students are at an early stage of developing a text and teachers want to focus their feedback primarily on content rather than language but also note a couple of problematic patterns in the texts for the student to be aware of during revision, the teacher might employ selective error feedback. In contrast, if students are in the final stages of producing a text and teachers want to show them the need for carefully proofreading and editing an entire piece of writing, they might provide more comprehensive feedback.

Errors versus Style

Second, teachers need to distinguish in their own minds and in their marking strategies between *errors* and *stylistic differences*. Because L2 writing teachers are usually either native speakers of English or highly proficient non-native speakers, as readers they are likely to be sensitive not only to morphological, lexical, syntactic, and mechanical errors, but also to wording that could be improved or wording or phrasing that is not exactly wrong but not precisely the way a native speaker might say it, either. Nonetheless, it is probably best for teachers to focus most of their efforts in marking and teaching on errors rather than improvement of writing style, except for very advanced students who make few errors. With a few exceptions (for instance, when to use active and passive voice or informal pronoun usage [e.g., *one* vs. *you*]), precise and effective writing style more likely comes from exposure to the target language (especially written language) than from correction or classroom instruction. (See Chapter 6 for discussion of how to further develop students' linguistic repertoires in the writing class.) When it comes to the specific issue of feedback on language in students' texts, teachers' energies are usually better spent on more explicit issues about which rules can be taught and learned and student progress can be observed. While in some instances the line between an error and a style distinction can be quite blurry, teachers need to be thoughtful in such cases about which items to mark and which to leave alone.

A related "style" issue is more philosophical than practical, and it comes from composition research that highlights the "appropriation" (taking over) of student texts that can occur when teachers become excessively hands-on in their error marking. Researchers such as Sommers (1982) and Brannon and Knoblauch (1982) discussed the harm—psychological or motivational—that can come to student writers when teachers, in pursuit of the "Ideal Text" (Brannon and Knoblauch), engage in behaviors such as crossing out words and phrases and rewriting them. Research on student views of teacher feedback (Straub, 1997) further suggested that students indeed resent such teacher appropriation, though a study focused exclusively on L2 writers (Ferris, 1995b) suggested that L2 students feel less strongly about this than do their monolingual peers. Notwithstanding an articulate rebuttal on the appropriation issue by Reid (1994), the point made by the earlier researchers is well taken: It can be off-putting and discouraging to students if teachers rewrite their texts, especially if the issues are stylistic rather than error-driven. Perhaps more important, such textual issues tend to be primarily idiomatic or idiosyncratic rather than patterned, so students may not learn much from those types of corrections, and teacher time devoted to them, therefore, is often not well spent.

Criteria for Selective Error Feedback

With these two points in mind—the occasional need for comprehensive error correction and the distinction between marking errors and marking for style—we turn our attention to the question of how teachers should select errors to mark in a given student text. Again, there are several options available to teachers depending on the larger instructional context (including course goals, point in the term, and so forth) and their own assessments of student needs.

Consider Errors Common to L2 Writers

While monolingual English speakers may struggle with issues such as punctuation rules, pronoun reference, and informal usage in their academic writing (Connors & Lunsford, 1988; Lunsford & Lunsford, 2008), L2 writers make a wider variety of errors. Though error types will obviously vary across student L1s, learner proficiency levels, and other student characteristics, the list of error types given in Figure 4.1 (taken from Ferris, 2006) is fairly representative of what researchers, teachers, and textbook authors have found and emphasized in giving error feedback to ESL writers.

In considering this list, or others like it, it is important to recognize several issues. First, errors made by students represent different types of linguistic knowledge. Figure 4.1 shows that the errors marked in this fairly large corpus were spread across morphological, lexical, syntactic, and mechanical categories. Truscott (1996) has argued that different types of errors may need varying treatment in terms of error correction, an issue often overlooked by teachers and textbook developers.

Recognize That Different Students May Make Distinct Types of Errors

A danger with lists of "common" ESL errors, such as that in Figure 4.1, is that they may be overgeneralized to all students. The types of errors that L2 students may make in their writing may be influenced by many different factors, including the amount and nature of English language learning or exposure to English that they have had (Ferris, 2009; Harklau, Losey, & Siegal, 1999; Roberge, Siegal, & Harklau, 2009), their current L2 proficiency (which may vary across lexical, syntactic, and morphological dimensions), and the influence of their par-

University ESL Students (mostly Generation 1.5) in California, Fall, 1998

1. Sentence structure
2. Word choice
3. Verb tense
4. Noun endings (singular/plural)
5. Verb form
6. Punctuation
7. Articles/determiners
8. Word form
9. Spelling
10. Run-ons
11. Pronouns
12. Subject-verb agreement
13. Fragments
14. Idiom
15. Informal

Figure 4.1   L2 Student Error Types (listed in order of frequency)

Source: Ferris, 2006, p. 103; adapted from Chaney, 1999, p. 20.

ticular L1s. In addition, of course, individual students will vary across motivation levels, learning styles, time and energy available, etc., but these types of individual variation patterns also occur in monolingual English speakers.

Students' English Language Learning Backgrounds

One of the most salient issues for teachers to consider is the nature of students' prior exposure to English. For U.S. writing instructors, it is important to recognize some crucial distinctions between international (visa) students and long-term U.S. residents (whether immigrant or native-born). As discussed in Chapter 1, international students are more likely to be "eye learners" (Reid, 1998a), meaning that their exposure to English has been largely formal, delivered through books and classroom instruction. Such students often have been educated with a strong English grammar foundation, have a good grasp of key grammatical terms (e.g., parts of speech or lexical categories), and can articulate rules. It should not, however, be assumed that this knowledge is always transferred accurately to student writing (or speech), as English language instruction in non–English speaking countries often falls short in providing opportunities for students to apply formal knowledge to their own written or oral production. International students who have a good "textbook" grasp of the basics of English grammar may benefit therefore from brief, focused reviews of issues most salient for English *writing* (as opposed to general overviews of English grammar) and from opportunities to practice and apply principles of grammar to their own writing. As this discussion relates to error feedback, students who, for instance, know what verbs are and understand the meanings and uses of different verb tenses may be able to take a code such as "vt" marked above a verb tense error and use it to access their previously learned knowledge to correct the error.

Resident immigrants, who include both late arrivals and early-arriving Generation 1.5 students, are more likely to be "ear learners," meaning that their primary exposure to English has been informal and oral (just as it was for monolingual English speakers). Their acquired grasp of what "sounds" right may help them to select lexical items more accurately and to produce more idiomatically appropriate sentences. On the other hand, they may have little or no formal knowledge of grammatical terms or rules. Unfortunately for this group of students, most editing handbooks for L2 student writers assume the international student's base of knowledge, starting, for instance, with rules for how to select the correct verb tense in discourse or how to avoid errors in subject-verb agreement, but overlooking the fact that some L2 students may not know the terms *verb, tense, subject,* or *agreement.* Indeed, in a recent study of Generation 1.5 college writers (Ferris et al., 2010), though students reported having been taught English grammar in secondary schools, they also said that they had failed to understand and/or retain that knowledge, and this lack of uptake was demonstrated in their writing and revision processes.

It is therefore vital that teachers of L2 writers take time to ascertain what their students know (or do not know) about formal grammar before adopting or utilizing any sort of error correction system. This can be done by means of a questionnaire and/or grammar knowledge pretest at the beginning of the course (see Ferris & Roberts, 2001, for a sample). This advance knowledge will help teachers to develop a system of giving feedback that is responsive to students' knowledge and to plan classroom lessons addressing gaps in knowledge (see Chapters 5–6).

The Influence of Specific L1s

A second important way in which students may differ from one another is in the influence of the L1 on their written production (and specifically on the errors they may make). Findings from contrastive analyses have suggested, for instance, that native speakers of Japanese may struggle with using English articles correctly, that Chinese speakers may have trouble with the English verb tense system, that Russian speakers may have difficulty with word order, and that Arabic and Spanish speakers may make errors in sentence boundaries.[1] While the incidence of such error types will undoubtedly vary across individual speakers of particular L1s, such generalizations have practical implications for teachers of L2 writers. For teachers of multilingual classes (as in many English-medium institutions), it is helpful to understand that not all students will make the same types of errors. Depending on the makeup of a particular class, teachers may give students error feedback that helps them understand the target language structure by referencing the native language system. EFL instructors in homogeneous classes may find it beneficial, if they are not already native or fluent speakers of the students' L1, to investigate the similarities and differences between the syntactic and morphological systems of the L1 and English, to use this knowledge to assess students' particular strengths and weaknesses, and to design feedback and instruction that addresses these specific areas of need.[2]

Differences in L2 Proficiency

Finally, teachers need to realize that differences in students' levels of L2 proficiency will affect both the number and type of errors that students make as well as their ability to process particular types of feedback. For an advanced international student or EFL learner, a cryptic code marked above an error such as "pl," "vt," etc., might be sufficient, depending on the student's prior instruction, to elicit an entire system of formally learned terms and rules. Students from the same L1, however, who are not very far along in either formal knowledge or language acquisition might be bewildered by such a mark, or, if they do understand it, unable to successfully correct the error. Brown (2007) provides a helpful taxonomy of the stages of error recognition and ability to correct through which learners may pass. At the "random" and "emergent" stages, learners are completely or partially unsystematic in their uses of particular structures. An example of this might be an Arabic learner struggling with English spelling. This student's bewildered teacher may notice that the same word may be spelled three or four different ways in the same paper (including even correct spelling some of the time). When students are at these pre-systematic stages, they are typically not able to self-correct their errors or even to provide a correction when the error is pointed out. At more proficient levels, which Brown terms the "systematic" and "stabilization" stages, students' errors are more systematic, showing clearly what they know and what they have not completely mastered, and students are able to correct errors either on their own or when pointed out by teachers.

Understanding these stages of development has practical implications for providing error feedback. For students at lower-proficiency levels, it may not be effective to simply locate an error (with or without a code or explanation) and ask the student to figure out the correct form. Instead, students may benefit from direct correction (defined in Chapter 2 and discussed further later)—the teacher providing the correct forms—and the opportunity to revise or recopy the text with the corrections inserted. This gives students needed input for acquisition, the "negative evidence" that some SLA researchers argue is necessary to prevent fossilization, and the opportunity to physically practice editing and correction of their own writing. In recent research, narrowly focused direct correction of this type has been demonstrated to aid learners' acquisition of the target forms (Bitchener & Knoch, 2010a, 2010b; Ellis et al., 2008; Sheen, 2007).

On the other hand, as students gain proficiency in English, it is important to give them feedback that will encourage, even require, them to analyze their errors and self-correct. While specific options and mechanisms for providing such indirect feedback are explained in detail later in this chapter, it is important at this point to remember both that students need a certain threshold amount of knowledge of English to understand and utilize this type of correction and that teachers should be intentionally moving their student writers toward self-sufficiency and independence as editors.

Decide How to Prioritize Error Feedback
for Individual Students

Once teachers know, in general, what types of errors their students might make, they will need to make some decisions about which errors to mark. There are three criteria that teachers can consider in making this decision:

1. Global versus Local Errors

SLA and error correction researchers have made a distinction between *global* errors—those that interfere with the overall message of the text—and *local* errors, which do not inhibit a reader's comprehension. These two examples illustrate the difference:

A. The tension was at its *pick*.

B. Last summer I *go* to visit my grandmother in L.A.

In Example A, the lexical error (using *pick* instead of the intended word, which was *peak)* could completely confound a reader. In B, on the other hand, the phrase *Last year* places the sentence into the correct time frame, making the verb tense error (*go* instead of *went)* relatively harmless.

While the global/local distinction is intuitively appealing to teachers, it should be noted that the relative "globalness" of an error varies substantially according to the surrounding context of the error. It would be an overstatement, for instance, to say that all lexical errors are global and all verb tense errors are local, as can be seen in Examples C and D:

C. San Francisco is a very *beauty* city.

D. I *study* English for four hours every day.

Example C is a lexical error (word form) because a noun was used when the adjective form was required. Nonetheless, few readers would be confused about its meaning. The tense of the verb *study* in Example D could be either correct or incorrect depending on the intended time frame of the statement, which might not be obvious from the surrounding context. Thus meaning (as to time frame) could be obscured if the writer indeed was describing an event in the past, potentially creating a global error that interferes with reader comprehension. Thus, in providing error feedback, teachers need to consider the relative seriousness of errors in their surrounding context, rather than isolating specifc types of errors as being global or local.

2. Frequent Errors

Another common way to prioritize error feedback is to focus on errors that individual students make frequently. There are two possible ways to approach this. One is to complete individualized error analyses for each student based on an early writing sample (see Figure 4.2 for a sample). Based on this information, the teacher can provide each student with feedback targeted to his or her greatest areas of weakness. For instance, if a student appears to omit plural and possessive endings on nouns with

Student Name: _____

Error Type	Total Number of Errors & Percent of Total
Missing or unnecessary word	9/35 25.7%
Noun plural or possessive (missing or incorrect)	6/35 17.1%
Verb tense errors	6/35 17.1%
Article errors	4/35 11.4%
Punctuation errors	4/35 11.4%
Subject-verb agreement	3/35 8.6%
Wrong word or word form	2/35 5.7%
Sentence fragment	1/35 2.9%

Most Serious Errors to Work on During This Course:
1. missing or unnecessary words
2. nouns (plurals, possessives, articles)
3. verbs (tense, subject-verb agreement)

Figure 4.2 Sample Error Analysis Form

relative frequency, the teacher may wish to focus on that error each time she or he provides feedback so that progress can be assessed (Ferris, 1995a). In addition, grammar instruction (whether for individuals, groups, or the entire class) can be designed based on these initial error analyses (see Chapter 5).

While early-term error analyses can be highly informative for the teacher (and very much appreciated by student writers), they are likely too time consuming for most teachers to do every time they read a set of student papers. In addition, students may very well make different types of errors on different assignments, either because they have made progress or because the text type they are producing calls for different types of constructions. Thus, the "problem areas" identified by analyses of diagnostic essays at the beginning of a course may not be the most significant issues on papers written later in the term (Ferris et al., 2010). Teachers need, therefore, to perform an on-the-spot error analysis each time they read a student text on which they are providing feedback. This can be as simple as reading the paper through quickly and identifying two or three frequent or serious patterns of error.

There is one important caveat to the advice regarding the frequency of student errors. Teachers can get caught up in simply counting certain error types and overreact to students' difficulties with particular structures, overlooking instances in which the writer used the structure correctly. For example, an engineering professor recently came to my department for advice about a Turkish graduate student who in his estimation did not understand the English article system and "leaves [articles] out." He wanted someone in our program to "sit down with her for an hour and talk about this." He also appended a paragraph from the student's text as an illustration.

However, a quick scan of the appended student text showed me that she actually used articles correctly more often than not. She had seven instances of omitted obligatory articles and fourteen correctly inserted articles. Of the seven omissions, most were connected to one specific technical phrase and its acronym. Rather than saying that the student does not understand the English article system, it is more accurate to say that she was confused about its application in one specific instance. It would be helpful to remind her to monitor her use of articles (as she clearly does know the rules and can apply them correctly in many instances) and perhaps point out that one problematic construction. Teachers should thus read student writing carefully, not only looking for errors but also at what students did right, to get an accurate sense of the scope of the problem and the extent of the student writer's knowledge base.

3. Structures Discussed in Class

In providing error feedback, teachers may also want to target grammatical, morphological, lexical, or mechanical issues related to in-class work or out-of-class reading. For instance, if students are writing a personal narrative and analyzing why an experience was important to them, it might be helpful to focus on the use of different verb tenses in discourse (past tense to describe the experience; present tense to describe what they think today about the incident, etc.) and to give students feedback about their success or lack thereof in negotiating these tense shifts. If students are working on an assignment in which they are required to incorporate the words of other authors, teachers may wish to give feedback about the mechanical and syntactic issues that arise in the use of paraphrase and quotation. Such feedback may be particularly effective if the teacher has already provided some instruction about those specific issues; teachers' error feedback can then refer explicitly to this shared core of knowledge (see Reid, 1994). Chapters 5 and 6 provide detailed discussions of such in-class instruction; the point here is simply that one focus of teachers' corrective feedback could be reinforcing classroom instruction that has already taken place.

To summarize this subsection, instructors desiring to provide selective feedback on errors to their students have several different criteria to consider. The first, global versus local errors, focuses on the needs of the specific text being evaluated. The second, considering students' most frequent error types, reminds teachers that individual writers may have needs different from those of their peers, and these needs for feedback may change according to the task or as the course goes along. The final point focuses on what the class as a whole may be taught and how teacher feedback could be an effective follow-up to that language instruction. Any or all of these foci may be appropriate for an individual instructor's feedback efforts, depending on the design of the course and the characteristics of the student writers.

Timing of Error Correction

The timing of corrective feedback is an important and sometimes controversial question in the teaching of both spoken and written English. In considering spoken English, teachers must walk a fine line between lowering students' confidence and inhibiting their fluency and allowing errors in pronunciation, grammar, and vocabulary to "slip by" during class discussions or activities, perhaps misleading the students about what the correct forms really are. In teaching writing, many L1 and L2 composition theorists believe strongly that premature attention to error may short-circuit students' ability to think, compose, and revise their content. If teachers give too much error feedback early in the composing process (while students are still deciding what they want to say), students' further writing and revision becomes merely an exercise in proofreading rather than substantive thought (Sommers, 1982; Zamel, 1982, 1985). This danger is presumed to be especially salient to L2 writers, who are only too well aware of their linguistic limitations and thus more likely to focus on word- or sentence-level accuracy, to the detriment of the development of their ideas and improvement in written fluency.

However, other studies have suggested that L2 student writers are both willing and able to benefit from simultaneous feedback on content and form on the same draft of a text (e.g., Ashwell, 2000; Fathman & Whalley, 1990; Ferris, 1995b, 1997). One argument for providing at least some grammar feedback on all marked student drafts is that *not* doing so misses the opportunity to provide feedback at a teachable moment. Since many L2 student writers have significant accuracy problems, they arguably need all the input they can get from their teachers. By refusing to provide such feedback until the very last draft, teachers can severely limit these opportunities for needed input (see also Evans et al., 2010; Hartshorn et al., 2010). A compromise position is to provide general feedback about errors on preliminary drafts alongside comments about students' ideas and organization:

> *As you revise this paper, be sure to pay attention to your verb tenses and to the placement of commas in your sentences. I've underlined several examples of each type of error on the first page of your essay.*

On later drafts, the teacher can then shift the emphasis, providing more error feedback as needed. A related issue is whether error feedback is useful or necessary on final versions of student papers (i.e., papers that will not be revised further). Studies suggest that students are unlikely to go back and correct errors marked by the teacher when they have already completed the project and received a grade, and that such feedback, since students do not pay much attention to it, has little effect on their long-term development. Three possible pedagogical reasons for marking "final" drafts (perhaps by just highlighting or circling any remaining errors) are: (1) to facilitate charting of types/numbers of errors on essay drafts throughout the semester; (2) to communicate to students the need to proofread and edit future papers more carefully; or (3) if students will have the option to revise the paper further, for example, for a portfolio submitted at the end of the course. Another possible approach is for teachers to mark all remaining errors on final drafts and then ask students to correct and analyze their errors as a follow-up class or homework assignment. This final suggestion helps to ensure that teachers' time in providing corrective feedback is not wasted and that students will benefit more from the corrections.

Options for Corrective Feedback

The foregoing discussion of *which* errors to correct and *when* to correct them illustrates the range of options writing instructors have available to them in giving error feedback. These options are explained and illustrated in more detail in this section.

Option 1: Direct versus Indirect Feedback

As already noted in this chapter and in Chapter 2, previous researchers have argued for the superiority of *indirect error feedback*: indicating that an error has been made—through circling, underlining, highlighting, or otherwise marking an error at its location in a sentence, with or without a verbal rule reminder or an error code—and asking students to make corrections themselves. Indirect feedback, it is claimed (e.g., Lalande, 1982), forces students to be more reflective and analytical about their errors than if they simply transcribed teacher corrections (*direct error feedback*) into the next draft of their papers. Since students are required by indirect feedback to take more responsibility for their errors, they are likely to learn more from the process, to acquire the troublesome structures, and to make long-term progress in finding, correcting, and eventually avoiding errors.

In some of the recent corrective feedback studies discussed in Chapter 2, a strong case was made for the superiority of direct feedback over indirect feedback for student learning. However, in most of these studies, the goal was to assess students' increased accuracy over time in control of one or two narrowly drawn target structures (e.g., definite and indefinite article usage). In most writing contexts, teachers are more concerned with students' growth as writers and as strategic self-editors than with their increased control of a specific linguistic structure (an interest more characteristic of second language acquisition researchers than of writing specialists; see Ferris, 2010). Indirect feedback, especially if it is paired with required revision and/or analysis or reflection activities (see below and Chapter 5), has greater potential to help students grow in autonomy in monitoring their own writing. Two other pieces of research evidence support this argument for indirect error feedback in writing courses. First, in a longitudinal classroom-based study of teachers' error correction strategies and student progress in revision and over time, it was found that while direct error correction led to a higher percentage of correct *short-term revisions* (from one draft to the next), students who received more indirect feedback made more progress in *long-term written accuracy* (Ferris, 2006). Second, in studies where students have been asked to evaluate their options for receiving teacher error feedback, they have consistently opted for the indirect option, likely sensing that this would be most beneficial to them in the long run (e.g., Ferris, 2006; Ferris et al., 2010; Ferris & Roberts, 2001; Leki, 1991). In short, if the goal is sustained improvement in students' *writing strategies* (rather than measurable acquisition of specific structures), indirect error feedback is probably the best choice for teachers.

While indirect feedback clearly has more potential to influence long-term student learning and improvement in written accuracy, there are at least three distinct circumstances in which teachers should consider the judicious inclusion of direct feedback: (1) when students are at beginning levels of English language proficiency; (2) when errors are "untreatable," and (3) when the teacher wishes to focus student attention on particular error patterns but not others. Given these considerations, teachers may also choose to combine direct and indirect correction when they respond to student texts. Figure 4.3 shows a portion of a student text containing both direct and indirect error feedback.

As already noted, students who are in the early stages of learning English may not have either the formal linguistic knowledge or the acquired competence to self-correct errors even when their teachers point them out. Though it is unclear whether direct correction combined with student revision or recopying has a long-term effect on students' accuracy or their overall acquisition of these structures, producing well formed sentences after receiving error correction at least gives them input for acquisition; more important, it makes them aware from the early stages of the need to edit and correct their work.

sp
It is possible for some immigrants to be ~~truely~~ happy in America. The

immigrants choose to come over here, they are dreaming of a new, a

better life in America. The immigrants treat America as their home-
to
land. They hope ~~can~~ find happiness in here, and most of them find it.
wc   **vf**
Even they are not ~~truely~~ happy ~~in~~ here, ~~but~~ they still <u>being</u> so strong

to continue on the life road.

Figure 4.3   Student Text Portion with Direct and Indirect Feedback

Note: Only errors actually marked by the teacher are reproduced here.

Source: From Ferris (2006) research corpus.

Absent such feedback, students may fossilize or overestimate their knowledge and ability (Higgs & Clifford, 1982; Scarcella, 1996).

In addition to students' linguistic ability levels, the nature of the errors being considered may argue for direct correction. As already noted, a good proportion of the errors made by developing ESL writers are "untreatable," meaning that there is no rule to which students can turn to correct an error when it is pointed out to them. The most common errors of this type are errors in word choice, word form, and awkward or unidiomatic sentence structure. In such cases, it may be more helpful for the teacher to suggest a different word or a restatement of the sentence than to simply underline the word or sentence and mark "wc" (word choice) or "ss" (sentence structure). Again, by applying the corrections, students can receive some input for acquisition and a reminder of the need to select words and form sentences carefully. It also may be more effective to address more complex untreatable errors in a conference rather than through written feedback (discussed further later).

Finally, direct correction may be appropriate if the teacher desires to give feedback about an error but wishes the students to primarily focus their attention on some other pattern of error. For instance, a hypothetical student may, in an 800-word essay, make three errors in verb tense or form but 15 errors with plural endings on nouns. The teacher may choose to simply correct the three verb errors while giving indirect feedback on the noun plural errors so that the student can really pay attention to his or her most serious problem on that paper (perhaps even checking a learner dictionary or studying the relevant sections of a grammar/editing handbook on noun plurals). In short, while indirect feedback may have the most potential to help long-term student learning, direct feedback may have its legitimate role under certain circumstances.

Though direct feedback may be "easier" for the teacher and may please the students more in the short run (because it gives them the "right answer" and requires less effort on their part to make the corrections), overuse of direct feedback may also lead to teacher "appropriation" of the student text, as discussed previously. A potential danger of direct feedback is that the teacher, in providing the correction rather than guiding the writer to do his or her own editing, will misinterpret the student's original intent about what she or he wanted to say. Figure 4.4 shows an example of (in this author's opinion) overzealous teacher correction and its impact on the student's paper. This is not to say that a teacher should abdicate responsibility for giving students helpful error feedback (see Reid, 1994), but that direct feedback should be used with great care and only under the specific circumstances previously outlined.

One more elaborate form of direct correction is the technique known as *reformulation,* in which an instructor intentionally rewrites portions of student texts to provide models of how the language could work better in that specific context. Second language acquisition researchers have compared written reformulations to oral *recasts*, which adults often do naturally when interacting with young children (Child: "I goed to the park today." Parent: "You went to the park? Did you go down the slide?"), and which teachers also do with second language learners in classroom settings (e.g., Lyster & Ranta, 1997). However, the few studies that have examined reformulations of student writing as an alternative to other forms of corrective feedback have not demonstrated the effectiveness of the technique for student learning (e.g., Sachs & Polio, 2007). It is also worth noting that reformulation is an extraordinarily labor-intensive technique that also requires teachers to have a high degree of confidence that they are, in fact, correctly interpreting the student writer's intentions. For both practical and philosophical reasons, reformulation appears to be a correction option that is unlikely to achieve widespread acceptance.

Option 2: Error Location versus Error Labeling

Another decision teachers must make in marking student papers is whether to simply *locate* the presence of an error (by circling it, highlighting it, or putting a checkmark in the margin) or to *label* the types of errors that have been made,

Example A: Student Draft with Teacher Feedback:

> **adopts the new?**

An immigrant <u>practices their culture</u> within their community and as time go by the˄culture fades away.

old

Student Revision (next draft):

An immigrant practices their culture within their community and as time go by the old culture fades away.

Analysis: The student ignored the first correction and incorporated the second. Note that the first correction suggests a substantive change in the student's original content. However, the teacher's inclusion of a question mark may have indirectly given the student "permission" not to incorporate it.

Example B: Student Draft with Teacher Feedback:

The first reason that immigrants can't be truly happy in America is because they have to leave their country to start a new life. Every thing has to start over again. ~~Some people are forced to leave their country because of war or starvation~~. It is really sad for them to leave their country where they were born and lived for so many years.

Student Revision (next draft):

The first reason that immigrants can't be truly happy in America is because they have to leave their country to start a new life. Every thing has to start over again. It is really sad for them to leave their country where they were born and lived for so many years.

Analysis: In the earlier draft, the teacher simply crossed out an entire sentence without any explanation as to why he felt that the sentence was a problem or unnecessary. The student obediently deleted the sentence on his next draft. While the teacher may have had a good pedagogical or rhetorical reason for the suggestion to delete the sentence, this was not communicated to the student through this feedback.

Figure 4.4   Examples of a Teacher's Direct Feedback—and Its Results

Source: Ferris (2006) research corpus.

using symbols, codes, or verbal comments (see also Option 4). The primary argument for the former option (error location) is that it places maximum responsibility on the student writer to figure out both the nature of the problem and its solution. There is growing evidence that in many cases, L2 students, just like monolingual students, rely on their own acquired knowledge of the language to correct errors, only rarely relying on formally learned terminology and rules to solve problems. For instance, in the study by Ferris (2006), students were able to correct errors that were located but not labeled in 75 percent of the cases. More striking, when teachers coded errors *but used an incorrect code,* students were still able to successfully correct 62 percent of those errors, suggesting that, at least in those instances, they were relying on error location but not on (mis)labeling to make the correction. Results of a follow-up experimental study by Ferris and Roberts (2001) similarly suggested that there was no significant advantage for error labeling over simply underlining errors for students' ability to self-correct errors. Further, in a qualitative longitudinal multiple–case study, 10 L2 writers consistently identified their most reliable self-correction strategy as inserting the form that "sounds right" to them (Ferris et al., 2010).

The main reason to consider the labeling option is that it provides more information to the students so that they can call on their own prior knowledge or use resources such as grammar/editing handbooks to understand or remember the rule and figure out how to apply it. Error identification can be cumbersome for the teacher and confusing for the student. It is also fraught with possibilities for misidentification. Many teachers feel a lot more confident about their ability to simply locate errors than to accurately label the particular type of error that has been made. On the other hand, error identification could be especially salient and appropriate if it refers specifically to an already defined error pattern on which the student is focusing and/or to errors that have been covered during in-class instruction. Under these circumstances, the teacher can label errors with firsthand confidence that students should be able to access a specific knowledge system in response to the labels.

Several recent studies have added the variable of "meta-linguistic information" to their examinations of the effects of corrective feedback.[3] Some of the treatment groups in these studies received, in addition to text-specific corrections of error, explanations or rule reminders about the target structure being examined. These explanations were written in some cases (a sentence or two of brief instruction) and oral in others (five-minute, in-class lessons on the structure/rule). Students generally benefited more from corrections when accompanied by metalinguistic explanations, especially written information. However, these studies focused on only a few specific (and treatable) error categories, and it may not be as feasible for a teacher to provide such explanations when marking a range of more complex error types. Still, this recent research suggests that, where possible, providing a brief rule reminder at the point of correction may help student writers to process the correction more completely and effectively.

Option 3: Marking Broader versus Narrower Categories of Errors

If teachers are identifying or labelling specific patterns of student errors, another decision to be made is whether to use many smaller categories of error or several larger categories. The teachers in the Ferris (2006) study (see Figure 4.1) used the former system, marking some 15 different errors (not including the "miscellaneous" category). ESL editing textbooks are about evenly split in their approach to this question. Popular textbooks by Folse, Solomon, and Smith-Palinkas (2003); and Lane and Lange (1999); and the handbook by Raimes (2004) cover 20, 15, and 21 error categories, respectively, while texts by Fox (1992) and Ascher (1993) cover only five or six larger issues. For instance, teachers can mark and teach about "verb errors" (a large category) or break the treatment of verbs into several smaller categories, such as verb tense, verb form (which includes incorrect formation of the passive and errors related to modal usage), and subject-verb agreement. One can also talk about "noun errors" or about discrete errors in forming the plural or possessive, use of articles and other determiners, and pronoun-referent agreement.

The argument for using narrower categories in error feedback is that students can focus on a more limited range of forms and rules when learning about a specific error type. However, the use of 15–20 different terms or symbols to label errors may be overwhelming to teachers and students alike. Also, the distinctions between error categories are not always as precise as we may think. Teachers who are analyzing student errors or marking papers can have a hard time distinguishing between a verb tense and verb form error or determining whether a lexical error results from problems with word choice or spelling. A related reason for considering the use of larger categories of error in marking and teaching is that often smaller errors have the same underlying cause. For example, if a student omits an article or a plural marker when it is required, both errors may have the same root: a fundamental misunderstanding about the nature of nouns (count/non-count, abstract, collective, etc.). To summarize, the use of larger error categories may be preferable both because it is easier for teachers and students to deal with, and it may more accurately capture students' developing knowledge systems.

Option 4: Codes versus Symbols versus Verbal Comments

When teachers do choose to identify errors as part of indirect or direct correction, they must choose whether to use a set of error codes (see Figure 4.5 for an example), to use correction symbols (as copyeditors and printers do), or to use verbal cues to identify errors. Figure 4.6 shows how the same error could be marked in six different ways depending on which strategy is used. The argument for using codes or symbols is speed and efficiency: Teachers can write "vt" more quickly than "verb tense," and as they mark hundreds or even thousands of errors during a course, this labor-saving device is not insignificant! On the other hand, teachers who use codes or symbols must take extreme care to mark consistently and to

Error Type	*Abbreviation/Code*
Word choice	WC
Verb tense	VT
Verb form	VF
Word form	WF
Subject-verb agreement	SV
Articles	Art
Noun ending	N
Pronouns	Pr
Run-on	RO
Fragment	Frag
Punctuation	Punc
Spelling	Sp
Sentence structure	SS
Informal	Inf
Idiom	ID

Figure 4.5 Sample Error Codes

Note: Categories and codes taken from Ferris (2006) research corpus.

make certain that students understand what codes or symbols mean. Surveys of student reactions to teacher feedback have found that student writers resent cryptic codes or symbols that they do not understand (e.g., Ferris, 1995b; Straub, 1997). Some teachers, likewise, may find it more time consuming to learn, remember, and use a coding system consistently than to simply write the key word or term on a student's paper. Even when using complete words or phrases, though, the burden is on instructors to make sure that students understand what those references mean as well. Considering the example in Figure 4.6, if a student doesn't grasp the meaning of "verb tense" or know which tense to select under what circumstances, it won't much matter whether the teacher writes "vt," inserts a ^, or writes *tense* in the margin.

Option 5: Textual Corrections versus Endnotes

Another consideration facing teachers in marking errors is exactly *where* to place such marks. In most cases, the best place for error correction is at the specific point of error (as in

Original Text Portion: *I never needed to worry about my parents because they knew everything and could go anywhere they* **want.**

Correction Options:

wanted

1. Direct Correction: *...could go anywhere they* ~~want.~~

2. Error Location: *... could go anywhere they* <u>want</u>.

VT

3. Error Code: *...could go anywhere they* <u>want</u>.

4. Error Symbol: *...could go anywhere they* want_^_

tense

5. Verbal Cue: *...could go anywhere they* <u>want</u>.

6. Sample End Comment: *As you revise, be sure to check your verbs to see if they need to be in past or present tense. I have underlined some examples of verb tense errors throughout your paper so that you can see what I mean.*

Figure 4.6   Student Text Portion with Different Marking Strategies

most of the examples in Figure 4.6). However, a combination of error location (e.g., underlining) plus a verbal summary at the end of the paper or on a teacher feedback form may be very appropriate for advanced writers who are developing independent self-editing skills. In addition, if the teacher has implemented a program of tracking or charting student errors across drafts and assignments (see Chapter 5), a summary form that indicates the major errors marked and perhaps how many of each type there are may be a key component of the program. Another option made simpler by the increased use of electronic feedback is the insertion of brief rule reminders (metalinguistic explanations) in the margins using the Comments feature of a word processing program. Some instructors might even design macros for explanations related to common errors ("insert an article before a singular count noun" or "past tense form needed here") that could be placed in the text with a single keystroke. Others may find such technological innovations beyond them, may find that their explanations and corrections tend to be too idiosyncratic for generic macros, or may wonder to what degree students pay attention to and benefit from these comments. These are questions worth asking and researching further.

Option 6: Alternatives to Written Error Correction

There are several other ways that teachers can provide corrective feedback beyond the traditional ones already evaluated. One interesting approach was shared at the 2010 TESOL Convention by Dan Brown. Rather than underlining or coding errors or providing verbal rule reminders, he has developed a system of color-coding error patterns with highlighters—blue for verb errors, yellow for articles, green for word choice, and so forth. He spends time reviewing his fairly simple system (he uses only about five or six colors) with the students and then uses it consistently to mark student errors. Students can look through their papers to see how much blue is there (for example) and whether there is less blue than on their previous papers. Brown also reported on his follow-up surveys of students who had experienced this method, and they seemed to respond positively, saying that the color-coding made a more memorable impression on them than traditional written corrections had done in the past.

Another alternative to written error correction is the use of teacher-student conferences to discuss problematic language issues, particularly (as already noted) those that are complex and untreatable. In some instances, for example, a sentence may be so convoluted that the teacher is at a loss to understand what the student was trying to convey, let alone mark specific errors or even suggest a possible reformulation. However, error conferences have greater potential beyond simply unraveling problematic sentence structures. Completed thoughtfully, they can provide student writers with specific, on-the-spot input about language problems and allow them to ask questions and address points of confusion. A potentially even greater benefit is that teachers get a better sense of what individual writers understand (or don't) and of the types of strategies students use to choose language forms, to avoid errors, and to attempt to self-edit. This knowledge can in turn sharpen the teacher's future error feedback efforts and improve his or her in-class grammar and editing strategy instruction. In the study by Ferris et al. (2010), ten student writers were followed for a semester as they wrote four texts in class, received indirect, labeled feedback on their three to four most prevalent error patterns on each text, attempted to revise/edit those marked errors, and then discussed their errors and their editing processes in interviews with researchers at three separate intervals. Not only did all ten students show improvement in language control over time, but they and their instructor expressed great satisfaction with the combination of targeted, specific written error feedback and the opportunity to discuss it one-on-one with an expert. Though this procedure was designed for research purposes, we came away from the study asking how it could be adapted for regular classroom instruction.

As beneficial as error conferences can be, they are time consuming and challenging to do well. Suggested procedures for two different types of error conferences can be found in Ferris & Hedgcock (2005, p. 285). Because such conferences can go on for quite a long time if students write longer papers and/or make large numbers of errors, similar benefits may be obtained by discussing only a portion of the text with the student writer. Teachers may also decide to only do intensive error conference work with students who appear to most need it—either students who make a lot of different types of errors or those who make errors less likely to be treated effectively by written error feedback. That said, instructors should consider error conferences as a valuable alternative to written error correction when needed and feasible.

A final alternative (or set of alternatives) that should be considered is the various computer-based approaches to written error feedback. Brown's (2010) color-coding scheme is even more feasible if the teacher is responding electronically: Microsoft Word, for example, has 15 different highlighter colors and even more font colors. As already mentioned, the Comments feature (also in Word) allows teachers to highlight text and insert a marginal comment with a brief rule reminder or even a direct correction (e.g., about a lexical choice or suggested rephrasing). Some teachers use the Track Changes feature in Word to make changes (insertions and deletions), leaving a visual record for the student writer about what was changed; a related alternative is to ask the student to turn on Track Changes when revising or editing so that the teacher can see what steps the student took. In choosing any of these word processing tools to provide error feedback, the teacher will need to assess several related considerations: (1) the visual impact of the corrections (color-coding, Track Changes, etc.) on the student writer and (2) the teacher's comfort level in using these various tools—while Comments is fairly easy to use and modify, some find Track Changes visually annoying and hard to turn off, and some may find the process of selecting and highlighting/color-coding text to be more cumbersome than they would like. Teachers should keep their overall purposes and goals for providing correction firmly in mind before choosing and using any of these alternatives, but if they do so, one or more of them may be quite useful.

A more ambitious and complicated option is machine scoring or marking of student writing. Many teachers have heavy teaching loads (multiple classes and/or large class sizes) and wonder about the possibility of submitting student papers to an online marking/scoring program that will analyze textual features and in some instances, provide feedback on language errors and even rule reminders or explanations that have been tailored to the needs of L2 writers.[4] Crusan (2010) discusses such programs at length and offers these warnings:

1. There is not enough available research to assess whether such programs mark errors accurately (especially the errors made by L2 writers).
2. An even bigger question is whether student writers will be able to understand the error feedback and explanations these programs provide.

3. These programs are marketed under the assumption that response to student writing is a tedious burden rather than a dynamic interaction between a teacher and his or her students.

4. They also assume that teachers want to (or should) mark student errors comprehensively rather than selectively.

Crusan does acknowledge one potential—if limited—benefit of these automated analysis programs: Students could get more feedback than their teachers have time to provide, for example, if they want to do extra writing or additional drafts of an assignment. This is somewhat analogous to saying that student writers can benefit from multiple sources of human feedback (peers, self, tutors). If teachers encourage their students to utilize computer-based feedback programs (including word-processor based tools such as spelling and grammar check), they should also remind them not to accept such feedback uncritically or to use the computer as a substitute for thoughtful and engaged editing and rethinking of their own writing. Crusan (2010) concludes:

> It should be clear that machines that score students' writing, if used at all, ought to be used with care and constant teacher supervision and intervention. Presently, no clear evidence exists that machine scoring programs are able to handle the diversity of language produced by second language writers. I have seen L2 writers become very frustrated when faced with overwhelming feedback . . . . (p. 178)

Finally, an overreliance on electronic feedback will deprive teachers themselves of the benefits of analyzing and understanding their own students' needs, such as providing better feedback and tailoring classroom and individual instruction to students' specific levels of knowledge or confusion. In short, teachers of L2 writers should *not* look to computer programs to lessen their own responding workload and to "teach" their students about how to find and edit their own most serious and pervasive errors.

Following Up Corrective Feedback

As astutely noted by Truscott (1996), teacher choices and behaviors are only half of the equation in grammar feedback. If students do not or will not attend to error feedback, do not understand such feedback when they do pay attention it, or do not know how to incorporate it into their writing or to apply it to future writing tasks, the teacher's efforts will be in vain. Thus, it is important for teachers (and students) to perceive error feedback as part of a larger strategy of building students' knowledge and strategy bases, not simply a "fix-it" list for a particular paper. Students need to be made aware of the need to improve their accuracy and build their own self-editing skills, and they need to see how the teacher's feedback fits into the development of these abilities. (See Chapter 5 for specific suggestions on raising student awareness and motivation.) This, in turn, should encourage them to attend to teacher feedback when they receive it. Instructors can facilitate students' attention to accuracy by allowing (or requiring) students to rewrite texts after receiving error feedback, by allowing time in class for students to both ask questions and actually go over their teacher-marked drafts and make corrections, by training them in error correction strategies and pointing them to helpful resources (see Chapter 5; Ferris, 1995c; Reid, 1998a), and by holding them accountable through the grading scheme for making a good-faith effort to utilize teacher feedback and to improve in their own editing skills and overall accuracy of their texts. As already noted, teachers can also design follow-up tasks such as charting or error analysis that help students not only attend to teacher corrections but to utilize them for their own learning. Sample activities are discussed and modeled further in Chapter 5.

Avoiding Burnout

Writing teachers face a dilemma. They want to help their students to develop in every facet of their writing, including (and maybe even especially) their accuracy and control over standard written English. Yet responding to students' written errors can be time consuming and tedious. As an example, for a university ESL writing course I taught during the summer of 1998, I prepared individual error analyses for each of the 21 students, who had spent approximately 50 minutes in class writing diagnostic essays that ranged from about 400–800 words in length. Despite the fact that I am an experienced writing teacher and had done previous research involving error analysis (Ferris, 1995c), it took me 11 hours to complete the task. I found it a valuable exercise, and my students truly appreciated my efforts and felt that it helped them. But it was costly—and I certainly didn't keep it up for all of their subsequent papers!

This anecdote leads to a question that I am often asked when I give talks or conduct workshops on this topic: How can teachers possibly manage the workload—especially bearing in mind that many teachers have more, and larger, writing classes than I did? While there is unfortunately no "magic bullet" to make the process of giving error feedback incredibly fast or even moderately entertaining, a few suggestions can be offered to make the process of error feedback more efficient and satisfying:

1. **Do not feel that you must give written error feedback on every single paper students write.** Remember that teacher-student conferences (whether out of class or mini-conferences during class), peer feedback, and self-evaluation are legitimate and valuable alternatives for various phases of the writing process, including the editing phase (see Chapter 5; Ferris, 2003; Ferris & Hedgcock, 2005).

2. **Assess what your students know, find out what they want, and design your feedback strategies accordingly.** Once you have an idea of students' most common and serious errors, the level of formal knowledge of grammar that they possess, and their preferences with regard to error feedback, you can design a system of response that you can use consistently. As you and your students become comfortable

with the process of feedback and revision, the provision of error feedback should become less stressful and more efficient.

3. **Set realistic goals for error feedback.** Error correction should **not** be seen as the means to eradicate of all student errors but to encourage gradual but consistent improvement in accuracy over time, acquisition and application of linguistic knowledge, and development of effective self-editing strategies (see also Ferris, 2008).

4. **Make most of your feedback indirect, focused on error location rather than labeling, and verbal (not tied to codes or symbols).** Once you have established your priorities for feedback, the quickest way to move through student papers is with highlighter in hand (or on the computer), locating key errors so that students can go back and attempt to self-correct, and then adding a brief note about specific patterns of error to which students should attend.

5. **As time goes on, mark fewer errors and require the students to take increasing responsibility for their own progress.** This final strategy assumes that you are progressively training students to locate and identify errors, teaching them grammar rules they can use to address common errors, and giving them practice with sample and peers' texts in editing strategies (see Chapter 5; Bates, Lane, & Lange, 1993; Ferris, 1995c; Ferris & Hedgcock, 2005; Reid, 1998a).

Concluding Thoughts

The foregoing discussion has covered a number of issues and options for teachers to consider when providing error feedback to their students. The list of suggestions in Figure 4.7 summarizes these issues and assumes that error correction in L2 writing classes should be planned and executed carefully by the teacher and be part of a larger strategy for building students' editing skills (see also the Postscript at the end of this book).

Before Giving Feedback:
- Discover and consider what your students know—from prior language learning experience and your own instruction—about specific grammar terms and rules and about editing strategies.
- Ask students what **they** prefer: All errors marked or only the major ones? Error identified or merely located? A set of symbols or verbal feedback?
- Decide on your specific strategies: Will you mark all errors or only the most frequent/serious? Will you use indirect or direct feedback or a combination of both? Will you use codes, symbols, or verbal comments? Will you make corrections on the paper itself or give feedback separately (at the end or on a feedback form)?

While Giving Feedback
- Read the student text through quickly—*without marking it*—to determine what the most serious issues are.
- Check yourself to see whether you are being clear (and legible!) and consistent with terms, symbols, and other markings.
- Be careful that you don't mislabel an error—if you're not certain what type of error it is, look it up or just mark it without identifying it—and that you are focusing on *errors* rather than stylistic differences.

After Giving Feedback
- Be sure that students are clear about your error-marking strategies, including especially codes/symbols and grammar terminology, and that they also understand the principles of prioritizing and marking selectively.
- Give students time to ask you questions about their errors and to self-correct marked papers in class.
- Hold students accountable through the grading scheme for attempting to address your feedback.

Figure 4.7   Summary of Strategies for Error Feedback

In this chapter, I have overviewed many different questions and issues related to teacher correction of student errors. The fact that there are so many options to consider may be disappointing to some teachers, who may wish for a simple list of dos and don'ts that will work well for all students. But it is impossible and inappropriate to apply the same feedback strategies to all student populations and all situations. Only when instructors consider the needs, knowledge, and prior experience of students; make careful decisions about the goals and mechanics of error correction; embed error feedback in a larger context of developing knowledge; and build strategies that will improve student writing will such feedback have the desired effects in our students. Absent such careful decision-making, teachers might as well accept Truscott's (1996) argument that grammar correction is ineffective and should be abandoned.

Questions for Discussion and Application

1. As a teacher or prospective teacher, what is your view on the issue of *selective* error feedback versus *comprehensive* correction? Before reading this chapter, what would you have said, and what do you think now?

2. Imagine yourself (or remember) writing something in a second language. If someone were to correct your language errors, what would be most helpful to you—direct correction (the correct form provided) or indirect feedback (an indication that an error was made)—and why? Would you answer in the same way for novice L2 student writers? Why or why not?

3. If possible, obtain a sample from a L2 student writer that has some language errors. Read it through, and try to identify at least one error pattern (similar to the article issue raised in the example). Then do a quick analysis of how many times the student got the structure wrong and how many times he or she used it correctly. To what extent does this student appear to misunderstand the structure or the rule, and if this were your student, what kind of feedback or advice would you give him or her?

4. Look again at the discussion of alternatives to written error feedback. What are your thoughts about color-coding, in-person error conferences, or the use of word processing tools such as Comments or Track Changes?

Which one would you be most interested in trying (that you haven't done before) and why? Which appeals to you least and why?

5. Look at the discussion of using computer programs to analyze errors in student writing. If possible, look up one or more of the programs (see Chapter Note 4). Would you be interested in using one of these in your own teaching? Why or why not?

6. Examine the suggestions near the end of the chapter about how to avoid burnout in responding to students' written errors. Which one seems most helpful to you? Are there any that seem unhelpful, vague, or unrealistic?

Further Reading

These sources will help you go further in understanding the major themes developed in this chapter. Complete bibliographic information is provided in the References section at the end of the book. The list is presented alphabetically rather than chronologically or thematically.

Brannon, L., & Knoblauch, C. (1982).
Connors, R., & Lunsford, A.A. (1988).
Crusan, D. (2010).
Ferris, D.R. (2008).
Lunsford, A., & Lunsford, K. (2008).
Reid, J. (1994).
Sachs, R., & Polio, C. (2007).
Sheen, Y. (2007).
Warschauer, M., & Ware, P. (2006).
Zamel, V. (1985).

Appendix 4.1
Marked Student Papers with Analyses

Note: **Here are two sets of papers written by two different university ESL writers and marked by two different teachers. Each set includes a preliminary draft with the teacher's error markings reproduced, an analysis of the teacher's markings, the student's revised draft, and an analysis of each student's progress. A comparison of students/teachers is provided at the end of this appendix.**

Student 1—Draft A

Conflicts of Cultural and Languages Metamorphosis

Minorities are groups of people that have in common ethnic, racial, or religion, _{WF} _{WF} especially when ⓘ constitute a small quantity of a population. Minorities often have fewer rights and less power than majority groups. One reason of the existence of minorities is immigration. When culture and class difference between groups of people, it can cause inequalities or discrimination. Being a minority group affect a person identity in a negative way, specially when you are different in culture and race.

I grow up being a minority ~~group~~ in my native country Panama. "This affects a person's identity radically". I can say that for my experience. Just for being the minority group, most of the time you are the target of their criticism. If you get something well done they get jealous, in contrast they laugh. When you are the minority group you feel like in another world even though you are in the same country. You want to be accepted by them. You don't want to be a lonely wolf, you want to be in the pack of wolves.

I have to deal my Spanish at school and Chinese at home. It is hard to go on with this two different languages and culture. Usually when I'm outside or in my native country the people can't image that I'm Panamanian they judge the physical appearance. That gave me a lot of hard time, since child: Is the color of the skin so important?

"Who I am?", A Chinese or Panamanian? I have to find out some answers to so many

Note: Papers are from the Ferris 2006 research corpus and are used with student/teacher permission.

questions. I think that I'm both of them, Chinese and Panamanian. But if I have to

choose only one, I think is Chinese. (Because I have absorb the most part of the Chinese
 VF   FRAG
culture than Panamanian culture.) Being the minority isn't bad because you always

could get positive consequences from any kind of situation. I have the opportunity
                                                  growing up?
to experience more than one culture, however being grown up in the minority group
               RO
 VT?
feel confusing because your long-awaited feelings doesn't develop that suddenly.
                                   SP   SV
    In "A Story of Conflicts" Yeshia Aslanian describe about his internal conflict that
 VT   RO VT
happen when he was a child and when he came into the United States, he has to struggle
                                   SV
with the two languages and cultures, as I do. I have the Panamanian accent but just

by looking different it also affect me a little bit, because not only culture makes me a
         but
minority, Also my race is different from them. I often heard them saying something
        being   VT   VF
about me of Chinese people, but I'm Panamanian too. They don't realize that I born
                                         PR
there too. The way people look at you is somehow different. They only judge the
                                                        PR
external appearance, they just look the difference between and you and them. It is

like comparing a diamond to a diamond ring, a diamond is still a diamond with or

without the ring. But somehow people really cares if you wear a ring like them or

not...
                                        N   N
    Therefore, a minority group has to face many obstacle and after them, the reward

are satisfactory, like being bilingual, etc. However, a minority group is an easy target

of the inequalities and discrimination of people.

Analysis of teacher marking: This teacher was a voluntary participant in the Ferris

2006 study, meaning that she had agreed to mark all student papers comprehensively,

using the error-correction codes outlined in Figure 4.5. However, careful examination

of this student paper shows that her marking was far from comprehensive. A number

of language errors fitting the categories in Figure 4.5 were left unmarked. For instance,

in the first three sentences of the third paragraph, there are several verb tense errors that

the teacher did not mark, though she did note such errors elsewhere. When she did

use error codes, she appeared to stick closely with the codes provided (Fig. 4.5).

In addition, she added some direct corrections, particularly crossing out unnecessary

words, inserting missing words or suffixes, and suggesting rewordings in a couple of

spots.

Student 1—Draft B (revised)

Conflicts of Cultural and Languages Metamorphosis

Minorities are groups of people that have in common ethnicity, race, or religion, especially when they constitute a small quantity of a population. Minorities often have fewer rights and less power than majority groups. One reason of the existence of minorities is immigration. When culture and class difference between groups of people, it can cause inequalities or discrimination. Being a minority group affects a person's identity in a negative way, specially when you are different in culture and race.

I grow up being a minority in my native country Panama. This affects a person's identity radically. I can say that for my experience. Just for being the minority group, most of the time I am the target of their criticism. If I get something well done they get jealous, otherwise they laugh. When people are the minority group they feel like in another world even though they are in the same country. I want to be accepted by them. I don't want to be a lonely wolf, I want to be in the pack of wolves.

I have to deal my Spanish at school and Chinese at home. It is hard to go on with these two different languages and cultures. Usually when I'm outside or in my native country the people can't image that I'm Panamanian. They judge the physical appearance. That gave me a lot of hard time, since I was a child: Is the color of the skin so important? "Who I am?", A Chinese or Panamanian? I have to find out some answers to so many questions. I think that I'm both of them, Chinese and Panamanian. But if I have to choose only one, I think it is Chinese, because I have absorbed the most part of the Chinese culture than Panamanian culture.

It is true that everyone always could get positive consequences from any kind of circumstances, including being a minority. I have the opportunity to experience more than one culture, however growing up in the minority group feels confusing, because my long-awaited feelings don't develop that suddenly. It doesn't takes days to a person to realize who they are. It takes several months or even years to define who we are, especially being a minority.

In "A Story of Conflicts" Yeghia Aslanian describes about his internal conflict that happened when he was a child and when he came into the United States. He had to struggle with the two languages and cultures, as I do. I have the Panamanian accent but just by looking different it also affects me a little bit, because not only culture makes me a minority, but also my race is different from them. I often hear them saying something about me of Chinese people, but I'm Panamanian too. They don't realize that I was born there too. The way people look at me is somehow different. They only judge the external appearance; they just look at the difference between me and them. It is like comparing a diamond to a diamond ring, a diamond is still a diamond with or without the ring. But somehow people really care if you wear a ring like them or not…

Therefore, a minority group has to face many obstacle and after them, the reward are satisfactory, like being bilingual, etc. However, a minority group is an easy target of the inequalities and discrimination of people.

Analysis: The student successfully incorporated nearly all of the corrections, whether direct or indirect, indicated by the teacher on the previous draft. However, errors left unmarked by the teacher were not addressed by the student in the revision.

Student 2—Draft A

Identity is the qualities someone has that make him/her different from other people. A persons identity plays a bigger role in their life. No matter where we go, either going to church, school, or moving to another country, our identity reveals who we are. It shows that cultural, custom and language identify our identity [our?] [to others] [However,]. This identity is challenged when we come as a minority to a new culture.

One of the [se] challenges is trying to assimilate into the new culture. My own experience reveals these problems of assimilation. When I was in high school, I felt that the world was laying on my shoulders, just thinking of making new friends with the Americans. I had all sorts of questions that popped into my head, "Are they going to accept me because I have a brown skin, has [am] an accent, and ∅ [a] black hair." Also being able for me to have the perfect English to communicate, [in English] challenged me a lot. It motivated me to try harder. Since English is spoken language here, I needed to learn it. However, I felt that much like the author of "A Story of Conflicts." In this article, Yeghia Aslanian says, "I began to devote my self to Persian—reading, copying, and memorizing long stretches of Persian texts". Therefore, I have [I, too, have] hope that it [i] would lead me to success. Even today, I do feel that I do not belong here since I could [can] not communicate very well. I feel that part of my identity has been stripped from me. and it [I] was one of the sacrifice that I made when I moved here. However, it did not stop me from trying to learn to write and speak in English.

Another challenge facing a minority is coming into contact with an entirely new culture with different values. The culture in here is totally different than the one that I ~~was~~ accustomed to in the Philippines. ~~As~~ I observe ~~that~~ some teenagers here they do not have much respect for their parents and elders. In ~~addition~~ _fact_, they usually talk back to ~~their~~ _them_ ~~parents~~. I just could not imagine doing that to my parents. At the same time, _the_ Philippines is a conservative country while the U.S. is ~~a~~ modern country. However, I am in a different country and I have to open my eyes with all the new things that I am surrounded with like new culture, customs, and religion.

In addition ~~of~~ _to_ the challenge that a minority has to face is how much freedom they have in religion and speech ~~in~~ here. It shocked me. In the Philippines, we do not get that much freedom with these. ~~All I know is that~~ we just have to follow the rules and be numb to voice out? what we think is right to the government or else you will pay the consequences. Also, ~~how diverse~~ _is so diverse_ the U.S. ~~with~~ religion while _in_ the Philippines, they only see one religion, the Roman Catholic.

When we move to another country, we do not think that _it_ will become a minority. Therefore, our identity shows ~~of~~ who we are and we have to accept the challenges that we face as a minority, like learning the language and new culture.

Analysis of teacher marking: This instructor clearly abandoned the error-correction system agreed upon for the research project, ignoring the error codes and providing only direct correction. Again, his corrections were not comprehensive, as several problematic constructions are left unmarked (see the third sentence in paragraph two, for example). More striking is his arguably appropriative use of correction to change constructions that were not grammatically wrong to suit his own style preferences. Examples of this include the following.

Student's sentence: In *addition,* they usually talk back to *their parents.*
Teacher's correction: In *fact,* they usually talk back to *them.*

Even worse, the teacher at points provides direct corrections that actually lead the student to make an error.

Student's sentence: When we move to another country, we do not think that will become a minority.

Teacher's correction: . . . we do not think that *it* will become a minority.

Student 2—Draft B (revised)

Identity is the qualities someone has that make him/her different from other people. A persons identity plays a bigger role in their life. No matter where we go, either to church, school, or to another country, our identity reveals who we are. It shows our culture, custom and language to others. However, this identity is challenged when we come as a minority to a new culture.

One of these challenges is trying to assimilate into the new culture. My own experience reveals these problems of assimilation. When I was in high school, I felt that the world was laying on my shoulders, just thinking of making new friends with the Americans. I had all sorts of questions that popped into my head, "Are they going to accept me because I have a brown skin, an accent, and black hair." Also being able to communicate in English challenged me a lot. It motivated me to try harder. Since English is spoken here, I needed to learn it. However, I felt that much like the author of "A Story of Conflicts." In this article, Yeghia Aslanian says, "I began to devote my self to Persian—reading, copying, and memorizing long stretches of Persian texts." I, too, have hope that it would lead me to success. Even today, I feel that I do not belong here since I can not communicate very well. I feel that part of my identity has been stripped from me. It was one of the sacrifice that I made when I moved here. However, it did not stop me from trying to learn to write and speak in English.

Another challenge facing a minority is coming into contact with an entirely new culture with different values. The culture in here is totally different than the one that I was accustomed to in the Philippines. I observe some teenagers here do not have much respect for their parents and elders. In fact, they usually talk back to them. I just could not imagine doing that to my parents. Eventhough, the Philippines has a very different way of raising children, I realize now in a new country. Thus, I have to open my eyes to all the new things that I am surrounded with, like new culture, customs, and religion.

In addition to the challenge that a minority has to face is how much freedom they have in religion and speech here. It shocked me. In the Philippines, we do not get that much freedom with these. We just have to follow the rules and be numb to say what we think is right to the government or else you will pay the consequences. Also the U.S. is so diverse in religion while the Philippines, they only see one religion, the Roman Catholic.

When we move to another country, we do not think that it will become a minority. Our culture, customs, and language will be challenge when we are in a different country. Therefore, our identity shows who we are and we have to accept the challenges that we face as a minority, like learning the language and new culture.

Analysis: This student transferred virtually all of the teacher's direct corrections into his revision and did not correct errors left unmarked.

Comparison: Though the two teachers had radically different approaches to marking errors, the revision outcomes were similar: The two student writers made changes, mostly successfully, to nearly all of the items marked in the preliminary drafts. However, where errors were left unmarked, neither student independently initiated corrections.

One conclusion that could be drawn is that it matters little whether teachers use direct or indirect correction, since the revision outcomes appear to be the same. On the other hand, student 1 was forced to think about the error codes and provide the correct forms while student 2 merely had to copy what the teacher had provided. Other things being equal, it seems clear that student 1 is likely to learn and retain more from this correction-revision cycle than student 2. In fact, an independent longitudinal analysis completed by Ferris and Helt (2000) showed that the classmates of student 1 made substantially more progress in error reduction over the course of a semester than those of student 2. Further, the possible demotivating (or even confusing or frustrating) effects of the second teacher's appropriative correction behaviors should be considered.

CHAPTER 4 NOTES

1. For more information on contrastive rhetoric findings, see Kaplan (1966, 1987); Connor & Kaplan (1987).

2. While texts such as Swan and Smith's (2001) *Learner English* can be especially useful, even easily available resources like Wikipedia can give teachers a quick and accessible overview of specific languages and key elements of their structure and how they differ from English.

3. Recent studies examining the effects of metalinguistic explanation accompanying direct correction include Bitchener & Knoch (2010a); Ellis et al. (2008); and Sheen (2007).

4. Examples of machine scoring programs for essays cited by Crusan (2010) include MY Access!®, *e-rater*®, and Intelligent Essay Assessor™.

Chapter 5

Beyond Error Correction: Teaching Grammar and Self-Editing Strategies to L2 Student Writers

As already noted, teacher correction is not the only way in which instructors can "treat" student error and help them to improve the overall accuracy of their texts. Even Truscott, who opposes error correction in any form in L2 writing classes, acknowledged that there may be a legitimate role for strategy training and grammar instruction as an alternative means of helping students to edit their writing (Truscott, 1999). In this chapter, we will examine in some detail several important pedagogical issues and options related to treatment of student written error:

- the need to raise student awareness about the importance of editing
- the need to give students training in self-editing strategies
- the option of providing supplementary grammar instruction on problematic constructions through the use of in-class mini-lessons, grammar handbooks, etc.
- the option of utilizing peer- and self-editing workshops in conjunction with writing projects.

In this chapter, I will argue that all four of these options—used in conjunction with thoughtful and consistent teacher feedback strategies—may help students to edit individual papers more effectively and to improve in written accuracy over time. In addition, I will present a number of practical suggestions and tools that L2 writing instructors can use or adapt for their own specific contexts. The principles and suggestions in this chapter should be equally appropriate for specialized L2 writing courses and mainstream (mixed L1/L2) composition courses.

Helping Students Understand the Importance of Editing

As I noted in an earlier piece on this topic, "Though some teachers assume that all ESL students are obsessively concerned with grammar, to the detriment of developing and presenting their ideas, . . . many of my students have little interest in and pay limited attention to editing their work. They find editing tedious or unimportant, or they have become overly dependent on teachers or tutors to correct their work for them" (Ferris, 1995c, p. 18). This lack of interest, at least by some students, in focusing on editing may be attributed to two opposite reactions that L2 writers often receive from subject-matter instructors or even English writing instructors. On the one hand, subject-matter instructors may choose to focus only on students' ideas and mastery of course content, ignoring written language problems as unimportant to overall learning goals and/or excusing ESL writers' errors because of their language deficits compared with other students. It is certainly the right of instructors to privilege content over error in their feedback and grading schemes, and in many disciplines, it may be the most appropriate and humane approach. However, L2 writers need to understand that not all college/university instructors may be as understanding of errors, that there may be university-wide writing or graduation assessments that require a threshold level of accuracy for students to pass, and that future employers, colleagues, and clients in the "real world" may expect their writing to be clear, accurate, and in accordance with the usage conventions of standard written English.[1] L2 scholars such as Scarcella (1996, 2003) and Johns (1995) have written compellingly about the disadvantages L2 writers may face both in academia and in the workplace if they are not assisted with reaching basic standards of clarity and accuracy in writing (and in speech).[2]

In addition to these external, instrumental issues, instructors should also point out that written errors can interfere with the comprehensibility of the message. In other words, students, as well as teachers, need to abandon the idea that there is a true distinction between "content" and "form." In fact, it is often a false dichotomy. Content determines form (for instance, if the author intends to tell a story that happened in the past, the verb tenses will follow appropriately from that content-based decision), but lack of accurate forms can obscure ideas. Fairly accessible examples of this include errors in word choice and in verb tense. Teachers can easily demonstrate this to students by creating a handout for class analysis containing student sentences and/or essay excerpts in which student meaning is obscured or hidden altogether by errors in form.

On the other hand, students may appear uninterested in developing competence in self-editing because of a lack of confidence or even fear that has been instilled in them by previous English and subject-matter instructors. L2 writers speak of receiving comments from teachers like, "You really need to work on your grammar" or even "I will not read this paper until you correct the grammar mistakes." In surveys of student opinion about the importance of grammar feedback from writing instructors (Ferris & Roberts, 2001; Rennie, 2000), students typically respond that they feel they have serious grammar problems that impede the effectiveness of their writing and that they urgently need assistance from their teachers to produce accurate texts and to improve their linguistic control. In short, students feel overwhelmed by their own self-perceived lack of linguistic competence and by the negative feedback they may have received from previous instructors. The resulting lack of confidence may cause students to resist any attempt by teachers to help them develop self-editing strategies because they simply feel that they are not capable of finding and correcting their own errors.

Although these two opposite extremes in attitude—students' lack of interest in editing because linguistic accuracy seems irrelevant and their lack of confidence that they can improve without extensive teacher intervention—can be daunting for instructors to combat, they are not insurmountable problems. As to the first belief, that grammar and accuracy are unimportant, teachers can raise student consciousness in the following ways:

1. They can demonstrate to students that many people (subject-matter instructors, prospective employers, graduate programs) do indeed feel strongly about written accuracy in student writing. Two possibilities for conveying this point convincingly are to either prepare a simple summary of published research on "error gravity" or to conduct a brief survey of different subject-matter faculty on one's own campus in order to get a sense of how they view error in L2 student writing. A perhaps even more effective option would be to interview or survey local employers in some of the students' chosen fields (e.g., business, computer science, engineering) to see how they would perceive inaccurate and unclear writing by prospective employees who are non-native speakers of English.

2. Teachers should also address the very salient issue of graduation writing requirements at their institutions, if such exist. In many U.S. universities, students must pass an upper-division writing assessment (essay examination, portfolio, or writing course) in order to receive their degrees. In many, if not most cases, a grading rubric is utilized that includes linguistic control and the absence of serious or frequent errors as criteria that can affect the graduation requirement (see Figure 5.1). Teachers should discuss such assessments and

6 Demonstrates clear competence in development, organization, and sentence structure.
- Clearly addresses assignment with thoughtful thesis
- Is well organized and developed, using appropriate and effective details and analysis to support the thesis
- Demonstrates thorough understanding of the issues presented in the reading; documents sources of ideas and quotations
- Consistently uses language well; varied sentences and precise word choice
- Grammatical errors are rare and do not interfere with effectiveness of paper

5 Demonstrates competence in development, organization, and sentence structure but will have errors.
- Addresses assignment with clear thesis
- Is generally well organized and developed, using effective details and analysis to support thesis
- Demonstrates competent understanding of the issues presented in the reading; documents sources of ideas and quotations
- Generally uses language well; varied sentences and clear and appropriate word choice
- Grammatical errors may occur throughout but are not frequent and do not interfere with understanding

4 Demonstrates minimal competence in development, organization, and sentence structure but will have probably have weaknesses in one or more areas.
- Addresses assignment adequately with thesis, though it may be imprecisely worded or insufficiently focused
- Is adequately organized and developed, using details and analysis, though development may be thin at times
- Demonstrates adequate understanding of the issues presented in the reading; documents sources of ideas and quotations
- Uses language adequately: reasonable command of sentence structure and word choice
- May contain varied grammatical errors that do not interfere with understanding

3 Demonstrates developing competence in writing but remains flawed in development, organization, and/or language.
- May not respond adequately to the topic or be sufficiently focused
- May not be adequately organized or developed, be illogical, or have insufficient or inappropriate support for thesis
- May demonstrates lack of understanding of the issues presented in the reading; may fail to document sources of ideas or quotations
- May have an accumulation of errors in sentence structure and word choice and form
- May have an accumulation of grammatical errors; errors may interfere with understanding

2 Demonstrates serious problems in writing.
- Does not deal adequately with topic, may be off the point, unclear, or poorly focused
- May have serious problems with organization and development, use little or no detail, or have irrelevant specifics or unsupported generalizations
- May demonstrates serious misunderstanding of the issues presented in the reading; may fail to document sources of ideas or quotations
- May have serious and frequent errors in sentence structure and word choice and form
- May have an accumulation of serious grammatical errors which interfere with understanding

1 Demonstrates incompetence in writing.
- May be unfocused, confusing, or incoherent or completely misunderstand the issues presented in the reading
- May be severely underdeveloped
- May contain severe and persistent errors that interfere with understanding

---

Figure 5.1　Sample Grading Criteria for a University Writing Class

Source: Adapted from Department of English, California State University, Sacramento.

their grading criteria frankly with students, perhaps also showing them sample student texts that passed or failed the examinations primarily because of accuracy (or lack thereof).[3]

3. To address both issues (irrelevance and confidence), teachers should provide students with a "reality check" based on their own writing at the beginning of the course. At the beginning of the class, most instructors have access to one or both of the following samples of student writing: (a) a short, timed essay used by the institution to place students at the appropriate instructional level; or (b) a diagnostic essay written in class during the first week of instruction. Writing teachers should exploit this information both to assess students so that they (teachers) can plan instruction appropriately and so that students can have an accurate sense of their abilities at the beginning of the term. Students should be given "individual report forms" (as in Figure 4.2) that give them a sense of what types of errors they make and their relative frequency. This is the more negative part of the "reality check."

Reviewers of my previous work and even student teachers whom I have supervised have expressed concern, even alarm, about the prospect of handing students such a black-and-white quantitative assessment of their language problems in writing. Wouldn't it offend students, showing them that we are only on an obsessive "error hunt" and that we don't care about the quality of their ideas? Wouldn't it frighten them, demotivate them, and damage their already shaky self-confidence? While my response to this is admittedly anecdotal and not empirical, I can assert that both my own students and the students of the graduate tutors whom I supervise have decidedly *not* taken offense at receiving such reports; on the contrary, they have expressed profound gratitude not only for the detailed and specific information that the reports provided but for the effort and attention it required on the part of their teacher. Students over and over would make comments like, "My English teachers always told me to work on my grammar, but this is the first time anyone has ever told me *exactly* what kinds of problems I have."

The ten participants in our recent longitudinal multiple–case study (Ferris et al., 2010) echoed these sentiments; while they remembered having had grammar instruction in high school and (sometimes) receiving generic error feedback, they did not feel that this broad approach had helped them at all. On the contrary, several participants expressed some bitterness that they had ended up in a developmental ESL writing course in college, feeling that their secondary English teachers had let them down. If anything, I have found that attentive and concrete feedback creates a deep sense of trust in and respect for the writing teacher, believing that she or he cares about their progress and is willing and able to take labor-intensive steps to help them. In response to this demonstrated commitment by the teacher, students will often work harder than they might have otherwise.

This "reality check" can be profitably taken a step further and even promote student self-confidence. After reading students' placement or diagnostic essays, teachers can provide students with a two-step editing workshop that shows them how much they really can accomplish on their own (Ferris & Roberts, 2001). In the first step, students are given their original diagnostic essay back and asked to find and correct as many errors as they can during a given period of time (say 20 minutes). For the second phase, the teacher highlights remaining errors that students didn't find. The students are given the paper again and asked to try to correct as many of the errors marked by the teacher as possible.[4] The teacher then analyzes the students' success ratios in finding and correcting errors unassisted and then after feedback and returns the papers with an "editing report form." Though this editing process will require effort by both teacher and students and will consume some precious class time, it can have a powerful effect on student self-confidence. Students can observe firsthand that they really can self-edit their papers with fairly minimal teacher feedback (or even no feedback at all). This will not only help them to approach timed writing assessments with more confidence, but will also serve as a compelling argument for the use of indirect (rather than direct) feedback by the teacher. This exercise will clearly demonstrate for students that they really can learn to fend for themselves, at least to some extent, without excessive intervention by the teacher. Such a demonstration will likely be far more convincing than any explanation by the teacher about feedback procedures and may go a long way toward relieving student anxiety and frustration.

That said, teachers also should provide verbal explanations of their feedback and error treatment philosophies and procedures. Student survey research on teacher feedback has clearly indicated that students are aware of (or can be convinced of) the need for teacher response to focus on issues other than grammar or error, as long as error is *one* of the concerns of teacher feedback (Ferris, 1995b; Ferris & Roberts, 2001; Hedgcock & Lefkowitz, 1994; Rennie, 2000). Students also appear to understand, when it is presented reasonably to them, that it is to their benefit to learn to find and correct their own errors and that indirect teacher feedback can help them to do that as well as or better than direct feedback. Thus, teachers should explain from the outset *how and why* they will give feedback (on all aspects of writing, including errors) and should periodically remind students of their philosophies and practices. At the same time, they should balance their own beliefs with what students tell them about their needs and preferences for error feedback, considering student views as well (Ferris, 1995b; Reid, 2002).

In sum, there are several reasons why students may be reluctant to engage in self-editing tasks, and there are a number of steps teachers can take to combat the inertia, whether it stems from too much or too little confidence. It is important to think through approaches to raising students' consciousness and motivation about editing so that students will buy in to teacher feedback and other error-treatment strategies, but also, so that—and this is even more important—students will take the need for accuracy and editing seriously enough to put forth the substantial effort that long-term improvement will undoubtedly require.

Training Students in Self-Editing Strategies

Though there is considerable disagreement as to whether error feedback is helpful (see Chapters 1–2; Truscott, 1996) and whether grammar instruction benefits student writers (see Krashen, 1984), experts in L2 writing are unanimous that students need to develop self-editing skills and that classroom strategy training may well be useful to them.[5] Strategy training for developing self-editing ability could include the components listed on pages 130–141.

Helping Students Become Aware of Their Most Pervasive Error Patterns

As discussed in Chapter 4 (see especially Figure 4.2) and in the previous section, a detailed, comprehensive error analysis by the teacher can be an invaluable tool not only for the instructor but for individual student writers, giving them a clear-cut numerical sense of what their major issues are. In addition to this, if students have had previous L2 writing and grammar instruction, they may well have some fairly specific ideas about their areas of weakness. In Ferris and Roberts (2001), 72 university ESL writers were asked to identify from a list what their major grammar problems were, according to both their own assessment and/or what they had been told by previous English teachers. Their responses matched up identically with the patterns of error they produced in diagnostic essays written during the first week of the semester.

Educating Students about Principles of Successful Self-Editing

Students may, either from their own intuitions or from feedback from previous instructors, feel that all error is "bad" and that it is both necessary and possible to strive for error-free writing in a short period of time. They need to be informed of research that indicates that error is a natural part of language acquisition and that it may even signal progress, rather than deficiency, that steady improvement, not perfection, is the appropriate goal, and that language acquisition takes time and requires both effort and patience (Ferris, 2008). Figure 5.2 provides a list of understandable principles of editing that can be helpful in presenting these ideas to college-level ESL writers; other instructors may be able to add to these.

Teaching Specific Editing Strategies

Figure 5.2 also offers several specific pieces of advice about editing to give to students. The first, and perhaps the most crucial, is to remind students that they do need to make time for the editing phase, whether they are writing a paper outside of class or in a timed essay exam. Other ideas include reading the paper aloud (if possible); reading it from back-to-front (breaking the flow of ideas in this way sometimes helps writers to attend to language details rather than content); asking a friend to proofread the paper; and using the dictionary, grammar handbooks, and Internet resources and word processing tools such as spelling and grammar checkers wisely.

Training Students to Look at Problem Areas

When my daughter was an advanced student of Spanish as a second language in secondary school, she expressed frustration that she made a lot of errors in verb tenses when she wrote compositions in Spanish. I sat down with her with a draft of a paper and had her read it aloud, focusing only on the individual verbs. It turned out that there were only two sentences in her composition in which she had to worry about her verb tenses. With one sentence, she explained to me why the imperfect (rather than the simple past tense) was appropriate, and checked in her Spanish grammar book to see what the appropriate imperfect verb form was. In the second sentence, as I read it aloud to her, she heard that she had (erroneously) used the simple past tense and was able to make the correction. She found the whole issue of Spanish verb tenses much less

Definition of editing: looking over a paper you have already written to find and correct any errors in grammar, vocabulary, punctuation, or mechanics (spelling or capitalization).

GENERAL ADVICE:

1. Leave **plenty of time** to read over your papers. After you have written a paper, put it aside for an hour or two (even a day or two). If reading or editing on a screen is difficult for you, you may want to print out your draft and go over it with a pen or highlighter. Looking at your paper again with a clear mind will help you to find errors.

2. **Read your paper aloud.** This will help you to notice problems you might miss if you were reading silently and quickly. You might also try starting from the end of your paper and reading "backward"—read the last sentence, then the one before it, etc.

3. If you are using a computer, **run a spell-check** to catch any misspellings or typos. **But be careful!** The computer won't mark any mistakes that are "real" English words (for instance *their* instead of *there*). Also, **do not rely on the grammar checker!** It is designed for native speakers and is not programmed to catch errors made by ESL students. You will still need to proofread your paper yourself.

4. **Ask a friend to read your paper** and see if he or she notices any problems. But be careful—if your friend always corrects your errors, you won't learn how to find and correct problems by yourself. Also, be sure to also read the paper yourself—remember, your friend's advice could be wrong! [Even native speakers of English make grammar mistakes!]

5. Be aware of your own **individual error patterns,** and check your papers carefully for those problems. For instance, if you know you forget noun endings a lot, go through the paper and check all the nouns (a highlighter helps). If you're not sure of a particular grammar rule, check a textbook or ask a teacher, tutor, or friend for help.

6. **Be patient.** Learning grammar and writing skills in a second language takes time and effort. Don't expect to produce "perfect" papers right away! Keep track of your errors and work toward making fewer of them with each draft or new paper. Remember that you do **not** have to have a perfect, error-free paper to pass this class!

Figure 5.2   Strategies for Self-Editing: Sample Student Handout

overwhelming when she examined them verb-by-verb and realized that there were only two cases she really needed to think about and that she could solve her problem by reviewing what she had learned about verb tenses and checking forms in her Spanish book. In English writing (her first language), she was prone to comma-splice errors, but as I consistently reminded her to check for them, she greatly reduced the frequency of this error and could monitor for it when reminded.

With other student writers, as with my daughter, the task of self-editing feels much more manageable when students can prioritize ("I have trouble with articles and noun plurals but almost never with verb tenses, so I should check all my nouns carefully but not worry about the verbs") and make careful passes through a completed text to examine a particular issue. They can be easily trained to do this by means of exercises such as the one shown in Figure 5.3. It is helpful to do this type of editing exercise first through a whole-class demonstration with a sample student text. Then students can do peer-editing activities (discussed further later) in which they look only for specific structures to see if there are any problems, and then they can progress to self-editing their own texts for problems with particular target items.

Figure 5.4 shows an example of a class-, peer-, and self-editing workshop that can be used or adapted for L2 college writers at various levels of instruction.

Encouraging Students to Track Their Progress

As already noted, L2 writers may feel overwhelmed and intimidated by the challenge of reducing error frequencies and improving the overall accuracy and clarity of their writing. The consistent use of error logs or charts is one suggested mechanism for helping students to track and measure their progress (Ferris, 1995a, 1995c; Ferris & Hedgcock, 2005; Hendrickson, 1980; Lalande, 1982; Lane & Lange, 1999). As noted in Chapter 2, there has been little research done on the effectiveness of error logs as a pedagogical device, but the few studies that

Verb Tense Editing Exercise*

Read through the student essay and highlight or underline every verb or verb phrase. Some of the verbs have errors in tense. Circle the verbs you think have tense errors. Be prepared to explain to a partner why you think those verbs are incorrect and why the others are correct.

Children start learning how to write more from their parents than any other people. Therefore, parents are big influences on their kids. Children need their parents' encouragement. They also need a good environment to study in.

When I was a child, my parents spent their spare time helping me read newspapers. My father encouraged me to read by telling me that he wanted me to read all news. My father expected me to be good in school. He never forced me to read or write, but he always said, "Spending your spare time in reading and writing will help your knowledge improve." My father wanted to take me to the library every weekend. However, we lived in a poor country with few books and no public libraries. Therefore, my father took me to a small bookstore which was far away from my home. I started reading the Saigon news. Six months later, I realized that my reading had improve. This time I read by myself, and I don't wait until my father asked me to read. I volunteered to read for my father. One day he said, "Compared to other kids who are the same age as you, you are a very good kid because you are my good son." I was very happy when he said "because you are my good son." I promise myself that I would do whatever my father expected me to do. The way my parents influence me is very simple, but it's very important for me to take his advice to improve my reading.

In my experience, having a good place to study is very important. For myself, my father had create a good environment for me even though we live in a tiny house. He make a small table for me to read and write in a corner of the house. He said, "This is your private place to study. You can read and write whatever you feel like." My father not only made the table, but he also bought me some short stories to read.

These are the ways my parents influence my reading and writing. I believe it is unnecessary to have parents who have a high level of education. It is important how parents encourage their children.

Figure 5.3 Editing for Specific Forms or Error Types

*Note: This exercise assumes that students have had prior experience with identifying verbs and understanding the forms and usages of simple present, simple past, present perfect, and past perfect tenses.

Understanding Different Verb Tenses

Exercise 1: Look at this excerpt from the essay "Robo Teacher" (Kastorf, 1993). For each highlighted verb, complete the chart below. The first one is done for you.

1. I once **heard** my aunt, herself a teacher, speculate on why educators **refuse** to use computers to their full capacity. 2. She **said** many teachers **are** afraid that they would be eventually replaced by teaching machines.
3. This idea **interested** me, so over the years I **have watched** teachers to decide whether or not they could be replaced by robots. 4. My conclusion **is** that the best teachers could never possibly be replaced by machines, but to save money, the mediocre ones could be—in fact, should be—replaced.

Verb (Sentence #)	Tense	Explanation
heard (1)	Past	Talks about a one-time event (see the time signal "once")
refuse (1)		
said (2)		
are (2)		
interested (3)		
have watched (4)		
is (4)		

Exercise 2: Analyzing a Classmate's Verb Tense Usage. Exchange essays with a partner, using a piece of writing you have done recently.* With a pencil, circle each example you find of **present tense, past tense, or present perfect tense** (ignore other verb forms and tenses for now). Then complete the chart below just as you did in Exercise 1. **If you find any errors in verb tense, do NOT correct them. (You may discuss them with your partner in a few minutes.)**

Verb	Tense	Explanation

After you have completed the chart, spend a few minutes discussing it with your partner. See if the two of you can agree on (a) the tense of each verb you circled; and (b) an explanation for **why** that tense was used in that sentence. If you have any questions, discuss them with your teacher.

Exercise 3: Editing Your Own Writing. Using the information from your partner's chart (Exercise 2) and your follow-up discussion, go through your essay and make any corrections to verb tense (present, past, or present perfect) that you think are necessary. Then write a short paragraph explaining what you have learned (or remembered) about verb tense usage from this exercise.

Figure 5.4 Class-, Peer-, and Self-Editing Workshop

*Note: This particular editing exercise would obviously work best if the task elicited some kind of narrative requiring the use of the specified verb tenses. Teachers would want to design different editing activities for other task types.

	Error Ratios (# words divided by # errors in essay drafts)								
Essay/Draft	**1A**	**1B**	**2A**	**2B**	**3A**	**3B**	**4A**	**4B**	**Final**
Error Category									
Verb errors									
Noun ending errors									
Article errors									
Wrong word									
Sentence structure									

Figure 5.5 Sample Error Log

have been completed suggest that they are at least potentially beneficial consciousness-raising tools. In a qualitative case study that drew from a large quantitative text-analysis project (Ferris, 2006), Roberts (1999) identified a number of logistical problems associated with the error logs used in that particular study and suggested a number of ways that the process could have been improved, including better explanation and integration of the error logs into classroom procedures and using fewer error categories and codes. Figure 5.5 shows one sample error log scheme with a relatively small number of categories; this of course should be adapted for a teacher's unique syllabus and student needs. Even with these problems, students in class sections using error logs reduced their error ratios over a semester more than did students in paired sections (same class, same teacher) who did not maintain the charts (Ferris, 2006; Roberts, 1999).

A possible danger with using error logs is that students will focus on raw numbers alone and become either discouraged or complacent. To avoid these extremes, instructors need to discuss several issues with students:

1. As students improve in fluency and their texts become longer, they may make more total errors. Thus, students need to think in terms of *error frequency ratios* (total errors divided by total numbers of words) rather than simple error counts.

2. Various written genres may elicit different linguistic structures. Thus, students may, for example, have few problems in producing correct verb tenses in a personal narrative that requires mainly the use of commonly used tenses such as simple present, simple past, and present perfect. However, if asked to produce a text about a hypothetical situation in the future ("Imagine that it is the year 2050. What do you think the world would be like?"), they may make many verb errors as they struggle with unfamiliar future and conditional forms. Looking at error log counts, they could be alarmed by their apparent regression in their control of verb tenses without taking into account the complexity of the verb tenses called for by the writing task. In contrast, if a subsequent writing task again elicits simpler verb tenses, students may feel that they have made dramatic "improvements" when in fact problems remain in some areas.

3. Students also need to understand that steady overall progress in second language acquisition may lead to a more sophisticated writing style, resulting in student writers taking greater risks with both lexical choice and syntactic variety—and possibly an increase in raw error frequencies. It is easier to avoid errors when one produces simple, one-clause constructions with no subordination, no use of prepositional phrases and other adverbials, relative clause constructions, etc. Since instructors certainly do not want to discourage students from taking risks and developing a more mature writing style, they need to help students see that relative error frequencies are certainly not the only measure of high-quality writing. However, as a test-taking strategy, they may wish to suggest that students save "risky" uses of vocabulary and complex sentence structure for out-of-class multiple-drafting situations (when they can get feedback and revise) or for journal entries (when the goal is fluency and low-risk self-expression) rather than on in-class essay examinations.

Teaching Students How to Edit under Time Pressure

An unfortunate reality for many ESL college students in the United States is that they must pass timed essay examinations in order to pass their classes and/or to graduate. Though there are many reasons why L2 writers struggle to succeed in these situations (including addressing the writing task adequately, developing a topic and providing effective support, and organizing an essay successfully), the lack of linguistic accuracy that results when students have to produce written texts under stress (because of the high stakes) and under time pressure is clearly a major contributing factor to student failure in many contexts.

Thus, an important part of helping students develop successful editing strategies is to talk with them about what they can do when they have limited time and resources to proofread and edit their papers. To do this, teachers might utilize this process:

- Remind students that editing issues are included in the grading criteria for the exam and that they need to take them seriously.
- Talk with students about how they can/should manage their time during the exam (see Figure 5.6 for an example).
- Be sure that each student is aware of at least two or three individual patterns of error that he or she should monitor for when time is limited.
- Give them a few general pieces of advice (based on common ESL writing errors) that they can remember (see Figures 5.6 and 5.7).
- Consider "practice" timed editing activities (see the Editing Under Time Pressure exercise, Figure 5.7) on either sample student essays or on a draft of something they have already written.
- Build their proofreading and editing abilities throughout the course through the use of in-class editing workshops even for papers written out of class (see Figure 5.8). You can give them a personalized report afterward about their success ratios (as in Figure 5.8).

Note: The following schedule was suggested for a two-hour final examination in which students responded to an essay prompt derived from two readings they had previously completed and to which they were allowed to refer during the exam.

SUGGESTED SCHEDULE:
10 min.: Go over the question. Highlight key words and instructions.

10–15 min.: Plan your essay. Write a thesis statement and a brief outline of your supporting points, including information from the readings.

75 min.: Write your essay. Check your outline as you go along. Plan to write at least 4–6 well-developed paragraphs (10–15 minutes per paragraph).

20 min.: Proofread and edit your essay. Watch out for:
*missing words
*words you're not sure about
*missing noun or verb endings
*punctuation errors, especially with quotations
*verb tense problems

Figure 5.6 Sample Time-Management Plan for In-Class Essay Examination

---

Instructions: You will have exactly 20 minutes to proofread and edit the attached student essay. Imagine that you have written it during an exam and that you are now checking for errors before you turn it in. Read through the paper quickly, using the questions below as a guide. Mark and suggest a correction for any errors you find.

*Are there any spelling errors?
*Are there any words missing in the sentences?
*Are there any words used incorrectly? Can you suggest a better word or word form?
*Look at the nouns. Do they have the right singular or plural endings? Is an article needed? Has the right article been used?
*Look at the verbs. Do the verb endings agree with the subjects? Are the verbs in the right tense?
*Look at the punctuation. Do you see any problems with commas, periods, semi-colons, quotation marks, etc.?

Figure 5.7 Exercise for Editing under Time Pressure Exercise

Instructions: **Using the codes listed below, I have marked your errors in the five categories listed. You will have exactly 20 minutes to go through your paper and try to make as many corrections as you can, using the codes to help you understand what the error is.**

<u>Code</u>	<u>Meaning</u>
V	error in verb tense or form
NE	noun ending (plural or possessive) missing, unnecessary, or incorrect
Art	article or other determiner missing, unnecessary, or incorrect
WC	wrong word or word form
SS	sentence structure: missing or unnecessary words; wrong word order; run-ons and sentence fragments

Student Report Form: In-Class Editing Exercise

Student Name: _____

Error Type	Number of Errors	Number Corrected
V= Verb tense/form incorrect		
NE=Noun endings missing, unnecessary, or incorrect		
ART=Articles/Determiners missing, unnecessary, or incorrect		
WC=Word Choice or Word Form incorrect		
SS=Sentence Structure: Missing or Unnecessary Words, Word Order; Fragments; Run-Ons; Comma Splices		
Totals		

Figure 5.8 Sample In-Class Editing Exercise

Teachers should also, of course, work with students on other essay examination strategies, such as how to analyze a prompt and construct a working thesis and outline to follow while writing. Instructors (and students) need to be realistic, understanding that even in-class preparation and advice cannot solve the problems inherent in high-stakes timed writing assessments. Finally, whether instructors are grading their own students' timed writing or participating in group scoring sessions, they should in most instances be more tolerant of written errors in student in-class texts than they might be for out-of-class revised papers.

Providing Grammar Support

Another component integral to the treatment of error in L2 writing classes is focused grammar instruction. There is a fair amount of disagreement among second language acquisition researchers and writing experts as to whether or not classroom instruction in grammar, vocabulary, and other formal aspects of language is effective in building target language competence and improving the accuracy and clarity of linguistic output.[6] To the degree that there is consensus on the teaching of grammar in writing classes (see Frodesen & Holten, 2003), experts agree that it should have these characteristics:

- It should consist of brief mini-lessons, rather than extensive grammar presentations.
- Lessons should be narrowly focused (e.g., on the contrast between simple past and past perfect tenses rather than on all 12 English verb tense/aspect combinations).
- Topics for mini-lessons should be selected based on teacher (and perhaps student) analysis of class needs (as determined by detailed examination of student writing samples and/or by objective grammar/editing tests).
- Mini-lessons should always be explicitly connected to the students' own ongoing writing projects.

- Mini-lessons might include any or all of the following components: (1) "discovery" exercises (text analysis designed so that students can examine how the target language structures naturally occur in authentic discourse); (2) deductive presentation of key terms and rules with ample illustrations (sample sentences and text portions); (3) editing exercises in which students find, label, and suggest corrections for errors with the target construction; and (4) application activities in which students examine their own writing or the writing of their peers for correct and incorrect uses of the particular structure being studied.
- Because student needs in a given class may be varied, the teacher may present mini-lessons to the entire class, to small groups within the class, or even in one-on-one conferences with individual students.

A Sample Mini-Lesson Sequence

In two studies that my colleagues and I completed with L2 student writers who were two semesters below college level (Ferris, 2006; Ferris & Roberts, 2001), we found that many of the student writers had problems with selection and/or formation of appropriate verb tenses, other verb form issues (e.g., use of the passive voice), and subject-verb agreement. In this setting or in others like it, several different whole-class mini-lessons on verb tense and form might be beneficial. The sample sequence shown in Appendix 5.1 (pages 153–155) illustrates a mini-lesson that focuses students on tense shifts in written discourse between past and present tense. It assumes that students have a working knowledge of the term *verb* and that they have been introduced to the form, meaning, and use of simple past and simple present tenses. In Step 1, students are given a brief explanation of the need to maintain consistency in verb tense usage and to shift tenses appropriately, sometimes using time markers. A brief sample paragraph is used to illustrate these concepts. In Step 2, a discovery exercise, students examine the verb tense usage in an excerpt from an authentic text, simply labeling highlighted verb phrases as being either in past or present time, identifying the reasons for tense shifts, and underlining any time markers they find. They then extend this analysis to their own writing in Step 3, again simply analyzing tense usage (as opposed to editing for errors, though this may also happen in the course of the exercise). In Steps 4 and 5, they edit verb tense errors (past vs. present tense errors only) first in individual sentences and then in a student essay excerpt. The follow-ups to this lesson are lessons on use of the present and past perfect and then opportunities to pull the information together by peer- and self-editing texts for errors in verb tense usage.

The amount of time given to this sequence or others like it could vary depending on the needs of the student writers. If students are already well acquainted with the terminology and rules, they could spend most of their time applying their knowledge through focused passes at sample student texts, peers' writing, and their own papers. If they have had little or no grammar instruction before, the teacher could spend additional time going over the specifications of the various tenses and on discovery activities. Also, some of the practice exercises could be done as homework assignments with answer keys attached for self-study.

Mini-Lessons for "Untreatable" Errors

The verb tense lesson sequence discussed above is reasonably straightforward. Almost any reputable ESL grammar textbook will contain ample information to which teachers can refer in preparing brief explanations and practice exercises for their students. But what are teachers to do about the very pervasive and troubling error types—such as word choice and unidiomatic sentence structure—that have no rules students can apply to find, diagnose, and correct such errors and to avoid them in the future? In such cases, instructors can design mini-lessons that highlight strategies and resources students can use to avoid or monitor for errors if they are prone to making them. Appendix 5.2 (pages 156–159) shows such a sequence for word choice errors. It includes a brief definition with examples of "word choice errors" and then goes on to illustrate five "sources" of word choice errors (ranging from carelessness in proofreading to phonological interference). Practice exercises ask students to find word choice errors, identify what caused them, and suggest possible corrections. An "editing guide" provides suggestions about strategies for avoiding word choice errors in the students' own writing.

Selecting and Adapting Text Models for Mini-Lessons

As this discussion illustrates, the use of both published texts and sample student texts can be very helpful in designing grammar mini-lessons for the writing class. (They are valuable for illustrating many writing issues other than grammar, as well.) As with many other aspects of teaching writing, selection of text models for classroom instruction is not as simple as it may appear. For discovery activities that utilize authentic texts (i.e., not designed especially for the language class), it can be beneficial to (re-)use texts with which students are already familiar, for instance, a reading from a class textbook that they have already discussed. Prior knowledge of the content of the text helps students to process it better and thus to focus well on the target structure during the mini-lesson. If there is no such text available to illustrate the structure or issue clearly and adequately, another possible source is other reading or writing textbooks with texts at appropriate levels of difficulty. The text (or text portion) should be short and accessible, with vocabulary and concepts not so abstract or unfamiliar that meaning will impede students' ability to isolate the target constructions. Remember that the purpose of discovery exercises is to examine how the structure occurs naturally in authentic texts, not to build their reading comprehension skills.

Developing discovery or editing exercises based on sample student texts can be even more challenging. I have found several principles to be helpful in this process:

- Do not use texts written by students in the current class, as it may embarrass them or shake their confidence. Instead, with students' permission, make copies of student papers in a current class for use in a future class at the same or a similar level. It can also be valuable to trade student models with other instructors who teach students at equivalent levels of proficiency.

- Avoid student models that have numerous instances of word choice and sentence structure errors that render major portions of the text incomprehensible. Even if you are focusing on a very specific issue such as the use of articles, it can be very distracting to sort through confusing prose to find the target construction.

- If the mini-lesson is focusing on one particular issue or contrast, consider correcting other errors in the text that are unrelated to the main point of the lesson. This will help students to focus only on the structures relevant to that day's lesson. Alternatively, you can highlight or underline only the structures or errors you want students to analyze, as in Appendix 5.1, Steps 2 and 4, building their skills up to where they examine a text independent of such assistance (as in Step 5).

- Once you have helped students learn to isolate various error types through separate passes through a text, you may want to select a student text containing errors in several major, common categories so that they can learn to simultaneously edit papers for different problems, especially under time pressure (see instructions in Figures 5.6 and 5.7 as examples).

Providing Additional Resources for Self-Study

Teachers may find that student writing problems are fairly scattered and idiosyncratic and/or that some students may need additional information and practice on particular language structures. It can be helpful to make various resources available to students, including grammar/editing textbooks (e.g., Folse, Solomon, & Smith-Palinkas, 2003; Lane & Lange, 1999), editing handbooks (e.g., Raimes, 2004), a general purpose grammar textbook series, learner dictionaries, online resources, and packets of handouts and exercises, especially with sample student writing that features multiple examples of particular error types for students to examine and practice editing. Depending on resources available to teachers and students, they can make such materials available in a program library or computer lab, for purchase in the campus bookstore, or on a class or program website. Over the course of the semester, after the teacher has gotten to know the needs of individual student writers, it can be helpful to give them personalized grammar/editing assignments based on a required class handbook or other print or online materials.

Once teachers have selected additional resources and arranged to make them available to students, it can be productive to spend a bit of class time discussing how to use such tools effectively. For instance, the teacher can design exercises around a learner dictionary to help students understand how to use noun plurals and articles accurately by checking whether a noun is count or non-count. Student writers should also receive instruction (and warnings) about the uses and abuses of spell-check and grammar-check tools included on word processors and other online resources.

Under no circumstance should a writing class be turned primarily into a grammar class, as there are many other issues besides linguistic accuracy that are critical to students' writing development. Still, focused grammar instruction that targets specific writing problems and simultaneously teaches rules and editing strategies can be a key aspect of error treatment in the writing class. When it is combined with teacher feedback that is selective and consistent and with editing strategy training, it can give students the tools to eventually diagnose and solve many of their own writing problems.

Peer- and Self-Editing Workshops in the L2 Writing Class

In the foregoing discussion, I have made a number of passing references to peer- and self-editing activities as key components of strategy training and grammar mini-lessons. However, like teacher feedback and in-class grammar instruction, the inclusion of such activities is not without controversy in the L2 writing literature. Many writing instructors, even if they utilize peer response activities while students are drafting and revising the content of their texts, are leery of using peer response sessions at the editing phase of the writing process. The argument against it is simple: It appears (often to both students and teachers) to be "the blind leading the blind." L2 student writers by definition lack native-like control of linguistic structures, so how can they possibly be competent enough to give helpful error feedback to their peers?

While this argument is certainly compelling in and of itself, there are, in my opinion, several good reasons for implementing peer-editing workshops as part of an overall error treatment process, and there are also ways to limit and mitigate potential problems that may arise. The primary reason for using peer-editing as a technique should not be so that the peer editor can necessarily "fix" all of the problems in his or her partner's paper, but so that *readers* (the editors) can practice their own proofreading and editing skills. As I have noted elsewhere, "It seems to be true that it is easier to find mistakes in others' work than in one's own" (Ferris, 1995c, p. 19). This is why newspapers, publishers, and businesses employ copyeditors and proofreaders. It could be argued that students can also profitably obtain editing practice through exercises using sample student essays (i.e., not written by anyone in their class), and indeed, such activities are critical to the process of building editing strategy skills. However, it is more engaging and motivating to work on a peer's paper currently under construction than to always look only at models, especially because the author is usually working on the same general assignment that the editor is. It is also a better learning opportunity for both writers and editors to be able to discuss their findings, questions, and suggestions with each other. The writer of a sample student text cannot explain his or her choices to a peer editor, and this personal engagement can lead to a more productive experience. Thus, in conjunction with mini-lessons and strategy training, teachers can utilize a three-stage process (such as the one shown in Figure 5.4) in which students analyze model texts, then do peer-editing activities, and then do focused self-editing.

Problems with peer-editing—the related issues of students not knowing what to look for and/or giving incorrect or misleading feedback—can be minimized through careful structuring and supervision of peer-editing workshops. Most teachers find it ineffective to say, "Exchange papers with a partner and correct any errors you find." This task is simply too open-ended and inevitably it leads to some students marking things wrong that are not incorrect and missing problems that really are there. Then when the authors get their papers back, they are bewildered and frustrated with feedback that they do not understand or with which they disagree. To avoid such problems, students should be *trained* in peer-editing techniques, the workshops should be carefully *structured*, and the activities should be closely *supervised* by the teachers.

As already noted, it is most effective to use peer-editing as the second step of a three-stage process. Even prior to the first stage, the teacher may wish to discuss the value of such exercises with the students. This may be necessary to combat students' feelings of anxiety about either trusting peers to provide good feedback and/or about their own ability to self-edit their writing. Many students feel that only the teacher, not their peers and certainly not they themselves, can provide helpful editing feedback. To make the task feel more manageable, students should first look at a sample student text and try to identify errors related to particular structures. This exercise can be done either individually or in pairs or small groups, and should be debriefed with a whole-class discussion (perhaps with the text and highlighted errors projected on a screen). The instructor should help students not only to identify errors and to suggest corrections but especially to articulate explanations as to why a specific structure is correct or incorrect.

In the second stage, as students move to the actual peer-editing exercise, teachers can give them handouts or instructions that ask students to look only for specific types of errors in their partner's paper, ignoring any other problems they notice (or think they see). In Exercise 2 in Figure 5.4, for instance, peers are asked to examine their partner's use of verb tenses (both correct and incorrect) and to complete a chart with their analysis. They are specifically instructed, however, *not* to make any suggested corrections. In the follow-up self-editing stage (Exercise 3 in Figure 5.4), students use the information from their partner's chart to attempt corrections that appear to be necessary. During these in-class workshops, students should be encouraged to discuss any questions or disagreements, to articulate reasons or rules about why a structure is correct or incorrect, and to discuss possible alternatives to make the text more effective. They should also be allowed to ask the teacher for help in resolving questions or disagreements. The instructor may want to note questions that arise during peer-editing sessions that may be of general interest for an on-the-spot or future whole-class mini-lesson. If the teacher is actively engaged in monitoring peer-editing workshops, it can give him or her valuable information about the students' thought processes and about any aspects of language with which they are struggling.

Finally, the teacher should highlight the importance and value of peer- and self-editing activities by holding students accountable for doing a good job of completing them and of considering information from their partners. This can be done by asking students to submit peer-editing worksheets with final versions of their papers so that the teacher can assess both how helpful the peer editor was and whether the author grappled with the feedback he or she received. In addition, at the end of the workshop, students can be asked to write a one- or two-paragraph response to the editing activity in which they reflect on aspects of the workshop they found helpful, frustrating, or confusing, and on ways in which the feedback they received will impact their writing in the future (or at least on the next draft of the paper under consideration).

Again, neither teachers nor students should mislead themselves that peer- and self-editing activities will enable student writers to find and solve all of their writing problems. However, this is not really the point of such exercises—rather, they are an integral part of an overall plan by the teacher to raise students' awareness of particularly problematic structures and to build their editing strategy skills. As long as instructors (and their students) have realistic expectations, structure and monitor activities carefully, and use them consistently and in conjunction with other parts of error treatment (teacher feedback and mini-lessons), they can be extremely valuable. Perhaps most important, they can demystify the editing process and build students' confidence that they can cope with errors and their understanding that improving written accuracy is a process that requires patience, effort, and time.

Concluding Thoughts

The purpose of this chapter was to highlight ways in which L2 writing teachers can develop a comprehensive "error treatment plan" for addressing issues of linguistic accuracy in student writing. Studies of error correction in writing often highlight only teacher feedback as a means to help students improve the clarity of their writing. While error feedback can be a critical component of error treatment (see Chapter 4), it is not the only tool available to writing instructors. When teacher feedback is combined with strategy training, grammar mini-lessons, and peer- and self-editing workshops, it can provide a comprehensive approach that addresses different needs and individual learning styles and that leads students toward the ultimate goal of independent self-editing and improved overall writing. In the next chapter, we move beyond error treatment to the broader issue of developing students' academic language skills so that they have larger linguistic repertoires at their disposal as they write—which in turn, should help them to find, edit, and ultimately avoid errors in their writing.

Questions for Discussion and Application

1. The first section of this chapter argues that students need to be convinced of the importance of developing their self-editing skills. From your own experiences and observations, do you agree that this is true, or do you feel that L2 writers are already overly obsessed with sentence-level errors?

2. The same section gives several suggestions for providing students with a "reality check" or "wake-up" call about the effects of errors in their writing. What is your reaction to these suggestions?

3. As a writer and/or a teacher, have you ever tried any of the self-editing strategies suggested in this chapter? How well do you think they work for you and/or for students you have taught? Are there any caveats or exceptions you could mention? Are there additional or alternate strategies you could suggest?

4. What is your reaction to the suggestions in this chapter about preparing and delivering mini-lessons to L2 writers in your classes? How do they compare to more traditional approaches to grammar instruction you may have encountered or tried? What concerns or questions do you have about the idea of incorporating language-focused mini-lessons into a writing class?

5. This chapter acknowledges that peer-editing workshops for L2 writers are controversial but offers counterarguments and mitigating suggestions for incorporating them successfully. Were you convinced by any of these ideas, or do you think that peer-editing activities are too problematic to be worth the trouble?

6. Have you ever tried giving students individualized error analyses and/or having them chart their progress in reducing patterns of error? If so, how did those activities work for your students? If not, what questions or concerns do you have about incorporating these ideas?

Further Reading

These sources will help you go further in understanding the major themes developed in this chapter. Complete bibliographic information is provided in the References section at the end of the book. The list is presented alphabetically rather than chronologically or thematically.

Beason, L. (2001).
Eskey, D.E. (1983).
Ferris, D.R. (1995c).
Ferris, D.R. (2008).
Frodesen, J., & Holten, C. (2003).
Haswell, R.H. (1983).
Janopolous, M. (1992).
MacDonald, S.P. (2007).
Reid, J. (1998b).

Appendix 5.1
Mini-Lesson: Understanding Shifts from Present to Past Tense

1. Time Signals in Writing

Tenses occur in clusters (groups) according to the time frame (now, before now) of the text. A switch from the present-future cluster to the past cluster or the past cluster to the present-future cluster often goes along with a **time signal** (now, yesterday, last week, last year, soon) that helps the reader to understand that you are switching tenses.

Look at the example paragraph below and notice how the verb tenses change after the time markers (last year; Now that I am home).

I **don't like** traveling. I **think** traveling **is** expensive, tiring, and stressful, and expensive. But *last year,* before I **went** to London, I **thought** traveling to another country **would** be exciting and glamorous. *Now that I am home* from my trip, I **feel** differently.

2. Exercise: Examining Verb Tenses

Examine the 14 highlighted verb phrases in the paragraphs (from an essay entitled "Robo Teacher") below. Above each, say whether it refers to past time or to present-future time. When there is a switch from one cluster to another, try to explain the reasons for the switch. Also underline any time markers you find. **Note: Do not worry about separating the verbs into separate tenses such as "present perfect" or "past progressive." For now, just divide them into "past" versus "present-future" time.**

I once **heard** my aunt, herself a teacher, speculate on why educators **refuse** to use computers to their full capacity. She **said** many teachers **are** afraid that they would be eventually replaced by teaching machines.

This idea **interested** me, so over the years I **have watched** teachers to decide whether or not they could be replaced by robots. My conclusion **is** that the best teachers could never possibly be replaced by machines, but to save money, the mediocre° ones could be—in fact, should be—replaced.

It's easy to describe the replaceable teacher. This **is** the teacher whose most challenging task **is** to repeat everything in the textbook in front of the class. This teacher **begins** class by checking his lesson plan to see what page the class **is** on in The Book. He then **orders** us to take out our homework (questions from The Book **answered** in complete sentences) and to raise our hands if we **have had** problems answering any of the questions.

[Source of text excerpt: Kastorf (1993).]

3. Exercise: Examining Your Own Writing.

Look at the essay you wrote at the beginning of this chapter (or any other recent piece of writing you have done). Highlight all of the verb phrases and mark which ones are in the "present-future" or "past" cluster, as you did in Exercise 2 above. Also mark any time markers you find, especially those which signal a tense shift. [**Note:** Not all verb phrases will have tense markers. Just mark the ones you are sure are either "present-future" or "past."]

4. Exercise: Identifying Errors in Verb Tense.

Some of the sentences below contain errors in verb tense. If the tense of the highlighted verb is correct, write "C." If it is incorrect, write "I," try to explain why it is wrong, and suggest a correct form.

_____1. When I was shopping with my mother, I soon **discover** that people could tell that I was not one of them.

_____2. Sundara's aunt didn't want to her to date an American, but **wants** her to see a Khmer boy.

_____3. American culture **is** a mixture of many other cultures.

_____4. The clerk **is** rude when he spoke to my dad in a loud voice.

_____5. I told my dad I **know** where the nuts and bolts are.

_____6. As my father and I **walked** away from the counter, I started to hear the employees laughing at us.

_____7. As each day **goes** by, I was becoming more exposed to the other cultures in America.

_____8. I believe that it is not possible for immigrants to be truly happy in America if they **did** nothing to help themselves.

_____9. After he and his family came to America, he **dropped** out of school to help support his family for a while.

_____10. I **grow** up being a minority in my native country, Panama.

[Source of examples: Ferris (2006) research corpus. Used with permission.]

5. Exercise: Verb Tense Editing

Read through the student essay and highlight or underline every verb or verb phrase. Some of the verbs have errors in tense. Circle the verbs you think have tense errors. Be prepared to explain to a partner why you think those verbs are incorrect, while the others are correct.

Children start learning how to write more from their parents than any other people. Therefore, parents are big influences on their kids. Children need their parents' encouragement. They also need a good environment to study in.

When I was a child, my parents spent their spare time helping me read newspapers. My father encouraged me to read by telling me that he wanted me to read all news. My father expected me to be good in school. He never forced me to read or write, but he always said, "Spending your spare time in reading and writing will help your knowledge improve." My father wanted to take me to the library every weekend. However, we lived in a poor country with few books and no public libraries. Therefore, my father took me to a small bookstore which was far away from my home. I started reading the Saigon news. Six months later, I realized that my reading had improve. This time I read by myself, and I don't wait until my father asked me to read. I volunteered to read for my father. One day he said, "Compared to other kids who are the same age as you, you are a very good kid because you are my good son." I was very happy when he said "because you are my good son." I promise myself that I would do whatever my father expected me to do. The way my parents influence me is very simple, but it's very important for me to take his advice to improve my reading.

In my experience, having a good place to study is very important. For myself, my father had create a good environment for me even though we live in a tiny house. He make a small table for me to read and write in a corner of the house. He said, "This is your private place to study. You can read and write whatever you feel like." My father not only made the table, but he also bought me some short stories to read.

These are the ways my parents influence my reading and writing. I believe it is unnecessary to have parents who have a high level of education. It is important how parents encourage their children.

[Source of student essay: Ferris & Roberts (2001) research corpus. Used with permission.]

Appendix 5.2
Mini-Lesson on "Untreatable" Errors
in Word Choice

A. DEFINITION

1. ***Word Choice* errors** occur when either (a) the wrong word is used in a particular sentence; or (b) the wrong word form (for example, an adjective instead of a noun) is used.

   EXAMPLES:
   1a. I kept myself **concentrated** on my studies (should be **focused**).
   1b. I had to translate **to** him (should be **for**).
   2a. America is considered a melting pot, so being **multi-culture** would be a positive aspect in this country. [**culture** is a noun, but the adjective form, **cultural,** is required here.]
   2b. I can **communication** with my family by speaking Chinese. [**communication** is a noun, but the verb form, **communicate,** is required here.]

B. SOURCES OF WORD CHOICE ERRORS

1. Choosing the wrong word form (noun instead of adjective, etc.). [see 2a & 2b, above]

2. Choosing a word that has a similar meaning to the word you need, but which doesn't fit grammatically into the sentence [see 1a above—***concentrate*** and ***focus*** are similar in meaning, but while you can **focus yourself,** you cannot ***concentrate yourself.**]

3. Choosing the wrong preposition. [see 1b, above]

4. Choosing a word that **sounds like** the word you need, but which has a different meaning. ***Examples:***
   a. Because of my **flowing** English, people do not stare at me anymore [the writer meant **fluent**].
   b. At a wedding, the bride and groom **change their vowels** [should be **exchange their vows**].
   c. The tension was its **pick** [should be **peak**].

5. Not proofreading carefully and making "careless" errors in writing or typing. ***Examples:***
   a. Have you done your ***homeword*** [should be **homework**]?
   b. My parents never read books to **my** [should be **me**].

C. Practice Exercise 1

Examine the sentences below (word choice errors are highlighted). See if you can determine (a) the source of the error (see the list above) and (b) what a possible correction might be. Note: There may be more than one way to correct a particular error.

1. Before I came to America **for studying** for a bachelor's degree....

2. As **longer** as I live here, the more problems I find.

3. I was **educated** that class time is very serious and that telling jokes to teachers is not proper at that time.

4. Minorities are people that have in common **ethnic, racial**, or religion.

5. A **parent** language is **importance** because it affects a person's identity.

6. Not only has my cultural barrier been **coming alone**, but there are also other barriers that have an **affect** on my life as well.

7. People **immigrant** to another country....

8. Living without **dependent** on parents, I can build up more confidence and learn how to take care of myself.

9. In order for minority groups to **bind** into the United States, they must **accommodate** to the new culture.

10. They will **be** more opportunity **in** study....

D. Editing Guide: Avoiding Word Choice Errors

1. Be sure that you understand the differences between **noun, verb, adjective, and adverb** forms of different words (beauty, beautify, beautiful, beautifully) and which form to use in a particular sentence. **Strategy:** Determine what part of speech is appropriate for the sentence, then check a dictionary for the appropriate form.

2. For preposition errors, try checking a dictionary such as *Longman's* to see which prepositions go with particular verbs (look up the specific verb and see if there is any information about accompanying prepositions). If not, you may wish to ask a native speaker for help with this—prepositions can be very troublesome.

3. If you know that you make word choice errors because of hurrying and not proofreading carefully, be sure to leave enough time to read over your paper before turning it in—this is the type of error where reading aloud is very helpful.

4. Be careful when using a thesaurus (either a book or a computer version)—just because two words have similar meanings doesn't mean they can be used in exactly the same way in a sentence—remember **focus myself** but not ***concentrate myself.** If you are not sure you are using the word correctly and can't tell from the dictionary or thesaurus, ask a native speaker to help you. Rules like this can be very irregular and idiomatic.

5. Be especially careful about **sound-alike** word choice errors—these can be very confusing for a reader to figure out. If you are not sure you have selected the right word, don't just "guess" and put in a word that sounds like the one you want! Underline the word and check it in a dictionary or ask for help. If you are still not sure, it is better to rewrite the sentence to use a word that you **are** sure about!

F. Practice Exercise 2

The passages below have word choice errors of the various types we have discussed. See if you can find them, figure out what went wrong, and suggest a correction. There may be more than one word choice error in some passages.

1. Many people think that Muslims treat women bad.

2. He told me that because none of my two sisters didn't go to college, so he taught I was going to do the same thing as they did. At the beginning I was afraid because I didn't know nobody. In my country I never passed by this situation before.

3. The Americans humiliated me that I couldn't speak English as fluently as they were.

4. According from him, being a member of a minority had many positive and negative effects to his personal identity.

5. When I went to some Vietnamese party or wedding I could speak English to my relationship.

6. She worked as hard as she could to achieve an "A" average to meet people's expectations. While striking for her excellent in school she neglected the beauty of life.

7. However, in America, the Chinese were treated as a minority group where I was treated exactly the opposite comparing to my native country.

8. For example, my childhood experience was not fulfilled with happiness.

CHAPTER 5 NOTES

1. "Error gravity" research looks at the reactions of university professors in the disciplines or of professionals in workplace settings to errors in student writing (e.g., Beason, 2001; Hairston, 1981; Wall & Hull, 1989). Some of these studies have focused specifically on L2 writing errors (Janopolous, 1992; Santos, 1988; Vann, Lorenz, & Meyer, 1991; Vann, Meyer, & Lorenz, 1984).

2. For an early landmark treatment of this point about the expectations of real-world audiences, see also Shaughnessy (1977).

3. It is been observed to me that the reaction of L2 writing specialists to such high-stakes assessments should be resistance rather than accommodation to an inherently unfair system. I do not disagree with those views but rather feel that while L2 specialists are advocating for change, they nonetheless bear responsibility for helping students succeed under the requirements currently in place.

4. This procedure is similar, but not identical, to the "minimal marking" method discussed by Haswell (1983), who had used it in his freshman composition classes. Interestingly, his findings as to student success ratios in self-editing were quite similar to those of Ferris and Roberts (2001) nearly 20 years later, even though their participants were developmental ESL writers.

5. For views from a range of sources, see, for example, Bates, Lane, & Lange, 1993; Ferris, 1995a, 1995c, 1999b; Ferris & Hedgcock, 2005; James, 1998; Reid, 1998a; Truscott, 1999.

6. See, for example, Byrd & Reid, 1998; Doughty & Williams, 1998; Ferris, 1995c; Ferris & Hedgcock, 2005; Hartwell, 1985; James, 1998; Krashen, 1982, 1989.

Chapter 6

Beyond Error Treatment: Academic Language Development for L2 Writers

Throughout this book, we have proceeded on the assumption that accuracy and linguistic control are important issues for L2 writers, especially as to their long-term goals in academic and professional settings beyond the writing or language class. Thus far, we have focused on *errors* that L2 students produce while writing—what types of errors to mark, when and how to mark them, and teaching students strategies and rules for avoiding and editing their most problematic errors. However, retroactive error treatment should not be teachers' only approach to facilitating students' linguistic control in their writing. Rather, teachers should also be proactively helping students to analyze language, acquire or improve control of specific lexical and syntactic forms, and apply their knowledge to their ongoing writing projects. In short, *academic language development* should be the overarching goal, of which "treatment of error" is a part but not the whole.

In this final chapter, we will look at ways in which teachers can facilitate students' ongoing L2 acquisition within the specific context of a writing or literacy course. We begin with discussing the importance of intensive and extensive reading activities in this process, move on to ideas for helping students develop new knowledge about vocabulary and syntax, and end with suggestions for using the methods and findings of corpus linguistics research to promote ongoing language acquisition in the writing/literacy classroom.

Reading for Writers

The critical connection between reading and writing is well established in the L2 literature (Ferris, 2009; Ferris & Hedgcock, 2005; Hedgcock & Ferris, 2009; Hirvela, 2004; Krashen, 1985, 1988, 1989, 2004; Seymour & Walsh, 2006). Reading gives students ideas and content to write about, models rhetorical strategies and genre specifications, and provides extensive input for acquisition of vocabulary and syntax occurring within authentic discourse. It also provides examples of conventions particular to writing itself, such as paragraphing, capitalization, and punctuation usage, conventions that can vary across different languages.

Most L2 writing courses (or courses designed to promote L2 literacy in general) include some reading, and if they do not, they should. However, teachers tend to focus their selection criteria for assigned reading passages on providing content for writing assignments, promoting critical thinking, and engaging or motivating student writers. While these textual characteristics are all important, in at least some cases, teachers do not go far enough in either selecting texts for students or in fully "exploiting" them for classroom use. For example, a human interest story from a newspaper or magazine may be fun for students to read, discuss, and write about, but if the language of the piece is so simple that it does not adequately challenge students, it can be a missed opportunity to build students' linguistic repertoires. By the same token, even if a teacher selects a text that provides a model of challenging or varied language use, if students only talk about and examine the ideas in the text and do not look closely at how its language helps to accomplish the writer's rhetorical purpose, they again may be missing an important chance to practice analysis skills that could build both their reading comprehension and their active language knowledge for their own textual production. Thus, teachers should think carefully about their text selection and their use of required texts in the classroom, specifically and intentionally as a way of further developing students' linguistic knowledge.

Text Selection of Reading Material

Teachers should, of course, begin by selecting readings for their writing classes that facilitate the writing tasks being assigned (as to content and genre), that are an appropriate length, and that are (or could become) interesting and motivating for students. Beyond these basic criteria, instructors may wish to look more precisely at how language is used in those texts, with an eye to helping students analyze it productively and use that examination to build their own receptive and productive knowledge of the L2.

Analyzing Vocabulary in a Text

There are several useful ways in which teachers can assess the lexical choices within a text. First, especially for L2 writers, teachers should consider the *difficulty level* of the vocabulary. Research suggests that if even three percent of the vocabulary in a text is unfamiliar, the text can be difficult to the point of frustration for readers.[1] This difficulty level may in some instances be mitigated by readers' familiarity with the content and/or other extralinguistic information in the text (pictures, charts, typography, etc.), but in general, considering the proportion of unfamiliar vocabulary can be a good place to start.

Teachers of L2 readers and writers need also to be aware that there are least three distinct ways in which the vocabulary in an academic text can be challenging. First, of course, *jargon or topic-specific* lexical items can be a stumbling block if the content is not already familiar to the students. Second, *general academic vocabulary* that crosses disciplines and is outside of everyday conversation can pose a challenge—phrases such as *conduct an investigation* or words such as *examine* or *assert.*[2] Third, even general purpose, everyday vocabulary can cause difficulty within a text, especially if it is used in less common ways. For example, in an essay called "A Mason-Dixon Memory" (1997), author Clifton Davis tells a story of high school golfers gathering on the *putting green,* a noun phrase likely familiar to most English speakers with any exposure to golf, but one that could be confusing to a L2 learner who may recognize *putting* only as the present participle form of the verb *to put* and *green* only as a color.

Teachers have several options for examining vocabulary difficulty in a text. If they have access to an electronic version of a text, they can use a text analyzer such as the free Vocabulary Profiler within the Compleat Lexical Tutor (www.lextutor.ca), which provides an instant view of the proportions of words from everyday (General Service) word lists, the Academic Word List, and "off-list" words; highlights which words fall into each category; and yields type-token ratio statistics that indicate how frequently words are repeated and how many different lexical items are used within a text. If teachers do not have access to an electronic copy of the text, they can practice examining it themselves for words and phrases potentially unfamiliar to L2 readers and writers; ideally, they could even show it to current or former L2 students for their input on the difficulty level of the vocabulary. The goal of such analyses is not necessarily to exclude texts from course syllabi or from classroom activities but rather to help the teacher become aware, first, of ways in which a potential text could pose difficulties and, second, of specific lexical items that could become productive targets for in-class examination.

Examining Syntactic Structures in a Text

Extremely complex syntactic structures can make a text very challenging for L2 readers. For instance, if the subject noun phrase is distant from its predicate verb phrase, a sentence can be hard to process. Long, wordy sentences with a great deal of subordination and embedded phrases and clauses can also be difficult to follow. While teachers should be aware of such issues as possible barriers to *reading comprehension*—which in turn could lead to weak writing about that text—considering our topic of language development, teachers might also consider whether a particular text illustrates either a syntactic structure that they want students to gain more control over or one they want students to avoid overusing.

As an example of the former, some academic genres require skillful use of the passive voice, a construction that can be challenging for L2 learners to master and also one that Generation 1.5 learners who completed their secondary education in the U.S. may have been warned not to use by their English teachers. A teacher wishing to improve students' understanding of appropriate and active uses of the passive might notice that a text she or he is considering for the writing class syllabus contains many good examples of the passive construction.[3] On the other hand, an instructor wanting to help student writers write in "Plain English" (a style movement in legal circles[4]), or simply to avoid wordiness and out-of-control sentences in their writing, might choose a text with either long, complex sentences or shorter, elegant ones so that they can talk with students about ways to tighten up their own sentence construction.

Readability

Computer-generated readability formulas are based on both lexical and syntactic complexity within a text and can give teachers a quick general sense of the relative difficulty of that particular text. Readability estimates can be obtained easily if the text is in electronic form, either through using calculators included with word processors or through freely available websites.[5] While readability scores and vocabulary profiles are fairly general estimators of a text's difficulty, they can be a valuable starting point for a teacher's own analysis of a text and subsequent lesson planning. Again, they can help teachers avoid the pitfalls associated with selecting texts for student writers that are either too difficult or not challenging enough to promote students' language acquisition.

Analyzing Written Language for Style and Rhetorical Effectiveness

A final way in which thoughtful text selection and related classroom instruction can help student writers is by consideration of how an author's language choices help to convey his or her ideas clearly, persuade or influence a reader, and engage readers effectively. For example, in an opinion piece in a newspaper, blog, or website, teachers might direct their students' attention toward words and phrases that create an effect or convey the author's viewpoint succinctly or strongly. For instance, in an article opposing legalized same-sex marriage, Lisa Schiffren (1996) begins with the title "Gay Marriage, an Oxymoron." Analysis of the title alone can help students learn a valuable but not often used academic literary term (*oxymoron*), and having learned its meaning, they can instantly determine the author's stance toward the topic. Further, they can discuss differences between the word's denotation, or basic meaning (a word or phrase that is internally self-contradictory), and its connotation (the term is often used sarcastically as a way to denigrate whatever it refers to). In sum, with some thought during the text selection phase, teachers can easily and naturally provide students with opportunities to analyze language in authentic contexts, building both specific language knowledge and strategies that can be used for continued development. This student knowledge can, in turn, be used to produce more accurate and effective writing.

Designing Classroom Activities

Once a teacher has included language use as one of several interacting criteria for selecting assigned texts, students can be guided through the intensive reading process—pre-reading, reading, and post-reading phases—to attend to language along with content and other rhetorical features. For instance, as part of text previewing (before reading the entire text for content), students can be provided with and discuss a few key terms that might help them to comprehend the text better during the first reading. While reading, students can be asked to highlight or identify words and phrases in context that are new to them. After reading, they can in pairs or groups discuss the unfamiliar terms and come to an understanding of what they mean in those specific contexts. They can also, after reading the text once or twice for content and comprehension, be guided by the teacher to notice whatever linguistic features the teacher has decided to highlight. Figure 6.1 provides one example of such an activity.[6]

Instructions: Reread the three paragraphs below from May Sarton's essay, "The Rewards of Living a Solitary Life" (Sarton, 1974). Highlight each usage of the words *alone* **and** *lonely* **in these three paragraphs. How does the author distinguish between these two adjectives? How does her use of the distinction express her larger purpose in the essay as a whole?**

4. "Alone one is never lonely: the spirit adventures, walking/In a quiet garden, in a cool house, abiding single there."

5. Loneliness is most acutely felt with other people, for with others, even with a lover sometimes, we suffer from our differences of taste, temperament, mood. Human intercourse often demands that we soften the edge of perception, or withdraw at the very instant of personal truth for fear of hurting, or of being inappropriately present, which is to say naked, in a social situation. Alone we can afford to be wholly whatever we are, and to feel whatever we feel absolutely. That is a great luxury!

7. I am lonely only when I am overtired, when I have worked too long without a break, when for the time being I feel empty and need filling up. And I am lonely sometimes when I come back home after a lecture trip, when I have seen a lot of people and talked a lot, and am full to the brim with experience that needs to be sorted out.

Figure 6.1   Language Analysis Activity

Source: Sarton (1974); see also Hedgcock & Ferris, 2009; Spack, 2006.

There are several valuable purposes to such text-based language analysis activities. The first, of course, is that they facilitate reading comprehension, a goal whose importance is often underestimated by secondary and post-secondary writing instructors, who do not see "helping students read effectively" as part of their job description but rather assume (often wrongly) that if they assign a specific text, students will be able to read, understand, and write about it without any help. Second, such word- and sentence-level analysis may provide input for students' ongoing L2 acquisition. Simply reading a text for top-down comprehension of content does not ensure that students will understand, remember, and productively use the different linguistic structures to which they have been exposed. A more intentional classroom focus may help them attend to these features (including extralinguistic writing features such as punctuation) in ways that promote uptake and long-term acquisition. Finally, asking students to do language analysis activities in the context of authentic reading tasks may teach them valuable strategies that they can apply to other reading they may do outside of class or for other classes. This last goal is better achieved when students are explicitly taught vocabulary learning strategies (Coxhead, 2006; Folse, 2004, 2008) as a means to their continued long-term development. Simply doing exercises in class does not guarantee that students will retain them as transferable strategies for future learning. We will return to strategic vocabulary learning later in this chapter.

The Role of Extensive Reading

All of these suggestions apply specifically to what is called *intensive reading*, a term applied to teacher-selected materials and activities used by an entire class of students (see Aebersold & Field, 1997; Hedgcock & Ferris, 2009; Seymour & Walsh, 2006). However, where feasible, instructors should also consider incorporating *extensive reading* into their writing course syllabus. Extensive reading has been defined in various ways, but at its essence, it refers to having students read large quantities of material, ideally self-selected, primarily for meaning and enjoyment rather than for close analysis or classroom assessment.[7]

There is ample research in both L1 and L2 literacy studies that demonstrates the many varied benefits of extensive reading for learners and for ongoing L2 acquisition. There is also a great deal of evidence suggesting that strong, avid readers are much more likely to be successful writers than are those who do not read much or well (see Ferris & Hedgcock, 2005; Hirvela, 2004). Many aspects of English vocabulary and syntax are so idiosyncratic and idiomatic that, in all likelihood, the only way in which learners can gain understanding and control of them is through repeated and varied exposure to word uses and sentence structures in a wide range of authentic contexts. Extensive reading provides that exposure, in a sense for "free"—while readers are enjoying reading for meaning, they are also broadening their awareness of how the L2 works. Putting this discussion into the context of this particular chapter and this entire book, extensive reading helps to build student writers' linguistic repertoires so that they have more tools at their disposal as they construct texts—and more acquired intuitions about the L2 that can help them to monitor their own production and correct their own errors on the basis of what "sounds right," just as literate, educated native speakers do.

Reading for Language Development: A Summary

It may seem odd in a book on the treatment of error in L2 writing to include such an extended discussion of the role of reading in developing student writers' language control. However, the more I teach writing myself, assess student writing, and prepare new writing instructors, the more I am convinced that reading skills—particularly the lack thereof—are not only extremely neglected in composition circles but intrinsically important to every conceivable facet of teaching writing. Student writers with poor L2 reading skills may not be able to use source texts accurately and effectively (Folse, 2008; Schuemann, 2008), leading to muddled prose at one extreme and plagiarism at the other. Students who do not analyze language use during intensive reading experiences and/or who do not read extensively are likely to have limited control over language structures in their own writing. This inadequate control in turn leads to a range of writing problems, including errors in word choice and sentence structure (including collocations) or overly simple vocabulary usage and syntactic patterns, making writers sound unsophisticated, as in the text excerpt in Figure 6.2. "Sunny," the student writer, was an international student pursuing a master's degree in social work at a U.S. university. Her text shows lexical immaturity: She repeats the words *learn* and *study* in various forms numerous times in this short text. Nine of her vocabulary choices

First of all, boys and girls learn new things from different perspectives. Chapman states, "Boys and girls tend to have different styles of learning. Boys often dominate the classroom by competing to flaunt their knowledge or by creating disruptions. Girls sometimes feel more comfortable with cooperative learning than with individual competition." Take my personal experience, for example. I studied in all-girls high schools for six years. I enjoyed learning with my classmates a lot because when I learned new knowledge, I liked to discuss with my classmates. We shared our points of view and encouraged each other so I loved learning and got good scores. Moreover, most of my classmates passed the entrance exam of university which is only twenty percent passed rate that time. Thus, I believe that teenagers can more concentrate and enjoy in studying in single-sex schools.

Figure 6.2   Student Text Excerpt: Inadequate Lexical/Syntactic Development

are from the Academic Word List, but six of those nine came from the quoted source material. Most of her lexical items are from everyday conversational vocabulary. Further, when she does use advanced vocabulary or complex sentence structure, it more often than not leads to errors. While her paragraph is reasonably well framed, Sunny's language production suggests that writing adequate papers for graduate courses and a master's thesis may be very difficult for her.

In short, as we have been arguing throughout this book, L2 writers may fall short of reaching their academic and professional goals if their writing is inaccurate, imprecise, or immature. Their writing instructors thus have an obligation to help them make progress in language acquisition and especially improve language control in their own writing. A thoughtful approach to reading instruction—selection and teaching of texts for intensive reading and facilitating, encouraging, or even requiring extensive reading—is the first and arguably most important step to fulfilling that obligation. The next step after guiding students to *attend to* new language forms through reading and analysis activities is to help them *acquire* those forms and then later to *apply* them correctly and effectively to their own writing. It is to these practical concerns that we turn in the following sections.

Acquiring Vocabulary for Writing

If the development of reading skills is the most neglected topic in writing instruction, vocabulary development is a close runner-up. L2 writers will often self-identify "vocabulary" or "diction" as issues that weaken their texts, and writing assessment research suggests that lexical control can be a major contributor to the score given to a text by independent raters.[8] As already noted and discussed, word choice errors can severely weaken a text's effectiveness, to the point of incomprehensibility for the reader. Chapters 4 and 5 provide ideas as to how teachers can address errors in word choice in student writing.

Vocabulary Learning

Here we focus instead on how intentional vocabulary learning and vocabulary analysis can help to *improve a student's future writing*, in addition to helping the writer find and correct errors in current writing. As to vocabulary learning within the writing course, Folse (2008) makes a strong argument for building a thoughtful and systematic vocabulary instruction component into the syllabus. The eight points he raises and discusses are summarized in Figure 6.3. Readers interested in more detail about these suggestions are encouraged to read Folse's 2008 chapter and his excellent 2004 book, *Vocabulary Myths.*

The "Right" Vocabulary

Many of Folse's suggestions here are quite straightforward and speak for themselves. I do wish to elaborate on a couple of his points. Suggestion 2, "Teach the *right* vocabulary," returns us to some of the observations in the previous section on reading: That teachers should analyze texts that students are reading and writing tasks that are being assigned to obtain a sense of specific vocabulary items that could be most useful to their students at that particular point in time. Folse recommends that teachers become aware of the Academic Word List (Coxhead, 2000) and the University Word List (Xue & Nation,

1. Teach vocabulary.
2. Teach the *right* vocabulary.
3. Teach learners how to create their own lists of vocabulary that they need for writing.
4. Teach learners how to keep a vocabulary notebook that facilitates multiple retrievals of unknown or newly encountered vocabulary.
5. Teach collocations, not just single words.
6. Test vocabulary. Hold learners accountable.
7. Teach paraphrasing and summarizing.
8. Make sure that explicit teaching of vocabulary is included in the writing program from the lowest levels of language proficiency.

Figure 6.3   Folse's Eight Suggestions for Vocabulary Instruction in a Writing Course

Source: Folse (2008, pp. 9–15).

1984) as starting points for selecting vocabulary to present in class.

While these lists are indeed useful and readily available online, teachers and students may become overwhelmed by the notion of sorting through and learning, for example, the 570 word families included in the AWL. There are, however, a couple of shortcuts that teachers can use to decide which items from the AWL to teach explicitly. First, the AWL itself is divided into ten subsections, starting with the most frequent ten percent of words in the academic corpus. Teachers may wish to focus on earlier or later sublists depending on their sense of what students already know and what might be most useful for their writing. Second, another online tool, the AWL Highlighter,[9] allows teachers or students to upload or paste electronic texts and designate how many sublists of the AWL should be included. The tool then highlights all instances of AWL words included in the chosen sublevel(s), allowing students to see how the AWL term is used in context and how frequently AWL words occur in the text.[10] The teacher might also use the AWL Highlighter tool to analyze various texts that will be covered in the course to generate a list of vocabulary to explicitly teach and test, per Folse's suggestions.

Collocations

Two of Folse's other suggestions, Suggestions 5 and 7 in Figure 6.3, are also worth further comment. Collocations in academic writing can be extremely difficult for L2 writers. For instance, in "Sunny's" text (Figure 6.2), she says in her last sentence, "I believe that teenagers can **more concentrate and enjoy in studying** in single-sex schools." There are at least two distinct collocation errors in this one sentence: (1) the misuse of the phrase *more concentrate . . . in studying* (ignoring for the moment the word-order error of *more concentrate* instead of *concentrate more*). If she had said *teenagers can concentrate more in single-sex schools*, or *teenagers can concentrate more on studying in single-sex schools*, either construction would have been clear and accurate; and (2) the misuse of the phrase *enjoy in studying*. Sunny shows a misunderstanding of the verb-gerund collocation *enjoy studying*, which would have been correct without the insertion of *in*.

Any teacher of L2 writers will instantly recognize that such collocation errors are rampant and very hard to explain or remediate. Compounding the problem is the fact that L2 students who primarily learned English in a classroom may have studied vocabulary forms in isolation, without learning or recognizing the ways in which vocabulary items (co)occur with others in a sentence. Students may have also been encouraged to consult thesaurses or learner dictionaries to find synonymms for overused lexical items, again without the information or awareness that synonymous forms may have different sets of collocations than the word or phrase they are replacing. Writing teachers thus, in presenting new vocabulary to students, must be careful to point out not just the word's semantic and syntactic properties but also the ways in which it occurs within other words and phrases in a sentence. Students should also be taught to attend to and record collocations as part of their own self-directed vocabulary learning (see Suggestions 3 and 4 of Folse's list in Figure 6.3).

Paraphrasing and Citation

Another point raised strongly by Folse is that what teachers sometimes think of as "plagiarism" in fact demonstrates student writers' inadequate lexical control, together with a lack of effective strategies for paraphrasing and summarizing the words of other authors and incorporating them skillfully into their own texts. He begins his chapter with an anecdote about a student whom he confronted about plagiarism. The student, surprised, replied, "I didn't plagiarize. I can't say these things in a better way." Folse, after pondering this, concluded, "The more I thought about what he had said about the limits of his vocabulary knowledge, the more I was inclined to agree with him: He couldn't express these ideas better than the original author had" (Folse, 2008, p. 2).

While not justifying the unattributed borrowing of other authors' ideas and exact phrases within student texts, Folse makes two important points. First, we may be asking L2 writers too much when we say that they must "use their own words" in discussing the ideas of other authors; paraphrasing is a complex skill that involves, first, accurate comprehension of the original and, second, the ability to render those ideas into alternate lexical and syntactic forms that are both accurate and effective. We need to recognize exactly how hard this can be. Also, teachers need to explicitly teach paraphrase, summary, and citation skills so that students can either improve their own paraphrases or at least attribute their sources properly. In another chapter in the same collection, Schuemann (2008) also argues that "teaching citation is [not] someone else's job" (p. 18) and offers further suggestions about how writing teachers can approach this in the classroom. Many writing handbooks and websites offer advice and even teaching materials for citation; our point here is to observe that the vocabulary limits of L2 writers make attention to these skills even more critical than they might be for other student writers.

Vocabulary Analysis

Some writing teachers may remain unconvinced that a systematic program of explicit teaching and assessment of vocabulary is an appropriate focus for a writing class. Others may agree that such instruction would be a good idea, but wonder how in the world they would find the time for it in a crowded composition syllabus. While vocabulary *teaching* might not be for everyone, developing students' *vocabulary analysis strategies*—including how to apply their learned knowledge to their own writing—can and should be a part of nearly every writing course that includes L2 students. Folse (2008) touched on vocabulary learning strategies in his eight suggestions (Figure 6.3) and discussed them in much more depth in his book-length work on vocabulary (Folse, 2004; see also Coxhead, 2006). In a recent book (Ferris, 2009), I condensed these authors' suggestions and reframed them for a L2 reading/writing course. They are reprinted here in Figure 6.4.

Though some of the suggestions are similar to those of Folse in Figure 6.3, the emphasis and approach is somewhat different: Rather than learning specific vocabulary items, writers are guided toward an increasingly nuanced view of how lexical

---

1. Explain the different types/registers of vocabulary found in academic discourse, using illustrations from word lists.
2. Teach students strategies for analyzing problematic vocabulary in course texts and in other texts they encounter in school.
3. Encourage or require students to supplement class instruction with self-directed vocabulary learning.
4. Discuss the importance of lexical variety and appropriate register choices in academic writing. Also raise student awareness about collocations and syntactic consequences of using synonyms.
5. Help students review their own writing to analyze and revise their vocabulary choices to improve accuracy, variety, and sophistication.

Figure 6.4   Steps Toward Vocabulary Analysis and Application for L2 Writing

---

Source: Adapted from Ferris, 2009, Figure 5.2, p. 108.

choices can impact their writing, a stronger ability to notice and analyze such choices in their reading, greater autonomy in vocabulary learning, and improved strategies for applying lexical items (words and collocations) to their own writing. In short, they are taught analysis skills and strategy rather than particular lexical items. Of course, Folse's suggestions about vocabulary teaching can also be used in combination with analysis skills; they are certainly complementary.

The first three items in Figure 6.4 have been discussed previously in this chapter or are fairly self-explanatory. As to Step 3, I would briefly note that students' self-directed vocabulary learning could encompass items encountered both in assigned (intensive) reading as well as self-selected (extensive) reading. As for Step 4, calling students' attention to lexical and syntactic variety as a style issue, some additional explanation and illustration might be in order. I am certainly not suggesting a return to the vocabulary learning of my own elementary school days, when the vocabulary list of the week was accompanied by the obligatory test on Friday and often with a contrived "writing" activity in which we were required to "compose" a brief narrative or individual sentences in which we "used the vocabulary words in context." Such activities seemed artificial to me even when I was ten years old, and I am not advising them now.

Analyzing Texts for Lexical Variety

I would suggest instead that teachers discuss the issue of stylistic variety with their students, perhaps contrasting a well-constructed authentic text (ideally one the students have already read for content) with a repetitive and overly simplistic student text. Another interesting way to present this contrast would be to analyze lexical differences between an authentic original text and a simplified version of the same text (e.g., a literary work that has been simplified for lower-level L2 learners). Students could be led through identifying key words and phrases and their synonyms. Having analyzed a text(s), students could observe which patterns they thought were more effective, and why.

Lexical Bundles

L2 writers with limited vocabulary may indeed repeat important words (nouns and verbs, in particular), causing their texts to sound dull or immature. However, on the opposite side of the "lexical variety" spectrum is recent helpful research on *lexical bundles* and how they occur in texts across different academic disciplines or genres. For example, Conrad (2008, p. 124) showed examples of how the bundle *it is important to* is used in texts from applied linguistics, biology, psychology, and marketing. Corpus linguistics research has identified a number of these lexical bundles, and Conrad (and others) have argued that helping students become more aware of and use these commonly occurring and even expected bundles will help their writing to sound more academic and sophisticated.[11] Conrad suggested that writing instructors focus on a small number of lexical bundles appropriate for each assignment, for instance, *have been shown to* or *studies have shown that* for tasks requiring students to summarize data from studies they have read (Conrad, 2008, pp. 134–135). Again, a valuable first step can be leading students through analyses of how these bundles occur within authentic academic texts.

Readers may at this point wonder if the previous subsections are internally contradictory. Is the notion of lexical bundles at odds with the point about lexical variety, and does teaching lexical bundles promote plagiarism? In my view, the discussions of analyzing lexical variety and lexical bundles are both necesssary for different reasons and are complementary rather than contradictory. Overuse of key nouns and verbs in a text *does* weaken writing style, and students should analyze more sophisticated alternatives to varying lexical choices, including synonyms, pronoun reference, anaphoric/cataphoric reference, and so forth. Skillful incorporation of academic-sounding lexical bundles *will* help students sound more like they belong in the academic discourse community of which they wish to be members—but the same bundle should not be repeated over and over in every sentence of a paragraph. As to the plagiarism question, no one could reasonably argue that

Instructions: Think of a restaurant you have liked (or any meal you have really enjoyed) and brainstorm a list of possible words and phrases you might use to describe the food if you were writing a review of the restaurant or meal.

Now look at the excerpt from an actual restaurant review published by *Zagat*. Do you think all of the words and phrases in quotation marks needed to be, or some they so commonly used that quotes are unnecessary? Is it "plagiarism" to use these terms without quotation marks or without attributing a source (if names were available)?

"At the top of any list for a power lunch or dinner," this "luxury" Downtowner is "as wonderful as you would expect from the Four Seasons," providing "superb" steak and "beautifully prepared" seafood served by an "impeccable" staff; the "elegant," "delightful" setting is conducive to "easy conversation," making it a fine "place to celebrate"—especially if someone else is "footing the bill"; P.S. opening at 6:30 AM for breakfast, it also serves a bar menu until midnight.

Figure 6.5   "Bundles" or "Plagiarism"?

Source of text: www.zagat.com.

phrases such as *studies have shown that* are copyrighted and owned by any author in particular. Classroom discussions of paraphrase, citation, and attribution must go well beyond the lexical bundle level. An easy and engaging exercise to help students distinguish between the notions of "lexical bundles" and "plagiarism," based on the popular *Zagat* restaurant review guides, is shown in Figure 6.5.

Evaluating and Editing Students' Own Texts

Once students have become more aware of some of the choices available to them, they can be encouraged to review a text they have already written, either one that will not be revised further or one that is in the final stages of editing. With a partner, they could look at what they have already written and look critically for ways in which they could improve the lexical choices in their existing text, whether by adding variety or incorporating a lexical bundle. This is a substantially different task than asking students to contrive a text solely for the purpose of practicing learned vocabulary items. It is similar to what experienced writers and editors do in the final stages of text production.

Once students have identified possible modifications they could make, an important next step is helping them to do so accurately and effectively and to evaluate their choices. For example, as an in-class activity or for homework, they could highlight words and phrases that they would like to edit and insert potential revisions. (This could be done on a computer or by hand; Track Changes on a word processor could also be utilized for this task.) Their peer reviewer and/or teacher should give them feedback about whether the proposed revisions are accurate and better than the original versions. Students unsure about specific words or phrases can also try the easy trick of typing the proposed item into the Google search engine: If they get few or no hits on that phrase, it may be a good indication that it's not an idiomatic construction (or it would appear in the search results as being commonly used) or that it is incorrect. The goal of this exercise is not simply to tinker with a particular text but rather to train student raters in the interrelated strategies of noticing how good writers use their lexical choices to improve their texts and thinking about how they can do so in their own writing. Over time, such awareness should sharpen their precision and improve their style in writing.

Syntactic Development

As we have already seen, vocabulary and grammar (including morphology, or word parts) are inextricable: new vocabulary items need to be learned not in isolation but with their accompanying syntactic information (including basic data such as grammatical categories and more complex information about various possible collocations). Conversely, the lexical choices made will in turn impact the syntactic structure of the phrase or sentence. That said, it is worthwhile to look specifically at grammatical development beyond the word level, as the issues and instructional approaches are distinct enough to warrant their own discussion.

First, a warning: Many recent articles and book chapters for writing instructors provide a few general insights about grammar in the writing class and then direct teachers to a blinding avalanche of substantial published research, corpus-based dictionaries, and corpus-informed reference grammars to make their own decisions about what grammatical structures to present to their classes. It was my hope and intention in this chapter *not* to do that but rather to present a concise summary of the most consistent data and best practices, organized into a lovely chart, that classroom teachers could then consult for syllabus and lesson planning.

Having read many of the sources on grammar for writers published over the past decade, I am now convinced that my "concise summary" and "lovely chart" vision was unrealistic. Instead, I agree with Byrd and Bunting's (2008) assessment that "where grammar is concerned, one size [does not] fit all" and that "we do not have one single all-purpose grammar of English but several overlapping and interlocking grammars that are characterized by particular subsets of grammar and vocabulary" (p. 62). In particular, researchers highlight three general contrasts that are extremely important for writing teachers to consider:

1. Spoken language is dramatically distinct from written language.
2. Academic written language is substantially different from written language in fiction or journalism.
3. Academic written language varies significantly across disciplines and to a lesser degree, within genres of the same discipline.

The first contrast is especially important for teachers whose students are resident immigrants or Generation 1.5 learners, as their written texts often sound overly conversational (Ferris,

2009; Reid, 1998a). As this generalization applies to syntactic choices in writing, teachers may wish to point out to students, for example, that sentences in academic writing tend to be longer than in conversation, or that incomplete sentences described in writing handbooks as "fragments" are frequent in conversation but usually not tolerated in most academic writing genres. The second point is important because many ESL/EFL and composition readers draw heavily from literary and journalistic sources because teachers and students find them more engaging than academic texts. While choosing engaging topics and texts *is* important for student readers and writers, it is also important to expose them to reading and analysis of texts like those they will encounter in other courses. The language of academic texts is measurably different (as to both vocabulary and syntax) from these popular texts. Finally, especially in courses focused on academic writing, it is important to acknowledge cross-disciplinary and cross-genre differences in conventions. All three of these generalizations suggest possible applications for the writing classroom.

Syntactic Structures for Analysis, Instruction, and Application

As already noted, if one reads even a fraction of the recent research on corpus-based research that identifies lexical and syntactic features in various text types and genres, it is easy to become overwhelmed with the information and the possibilities for classroom application. In a writing course in particular—one not more broadly focused on language development or even reading skills—the instructor must be extremely careful to (1) focus on syntactic issues that are directly relevant to students' immediate writing needs and (2) incorporate work on those structures in ways that are facilitative toward meeting the other goals of the writing course.

While there are many issues that writing instructors could focus on, several in particular emerge from the recent literature. These are summarized in Figure 6.6 and discussed further.

One striking finding from the landmark work by Biber et al. (1999) is that academic written discourse tends to include a

Structure	Comment	Citations
Nouns & their collocations	Academic texts are "noun heavy," and different noun forms require varying syntactic structures	Biber, 2006; Biber et al., 1999
Verbs & their distribution	There is a relatively narrow range of verbs used in academic discourse; "reporting verbs" are especially important	Biber et al., 1999; Schuemann, 2008
Verb tenses	The use of simple past or simple present tense in research articles can vary across disciplines.	Conrad, 1996, 2001
Passive voice	The passive voice is widely used in some genres and dispreferred in others.	Biber, 1988; Biber et al., 1999
Hedging structures	In some genres, being overly assertive and direct is inappropriate.	Hyland, 1994, 1998; Hyland & Milton, 1997
Markers of persuasion	Overt markers of persuasion are found in "everyday argument" but less so in academic argument.	Biber, 1988; Biber et al., 1999, 2002

Figure 6.6   Useful Syntactic Structures for Academic Writing Development

large proportion of nouns and that there are common affixes (mostly suffixes) used to form those nouns.[12] The ways in which the nouns are formed morphologically in turn affect the syntax of the sentence. For example:

1.   The *investigation* of these phenomena is crucial.

2.   *Investigating* these phenomena is crucial.

In Example 1, the noun is formed by adding the derivational suffix *–tion*, and in Example 2, the participle form of the verb *investigate* is used as a gerund (verbal noun). Either form is correct and appropriate here, but the important observation is that the use of the derived noun *investigation* requires other syntactic adjustments, specifically the additions of the definite article and the preposition. Though both nouns have the same root and the same semantic content, they do not function in identical ways syntactically. As this simple example demonstrates, analysis of noun phrases, their formation processes, and the syntactic functions around them can help student writers become more aware of the complexities of this heavily used feature in academic writing.

The next three items on the chart in Figure 6.6 are concerned with verbs and verb phrases. Biber et al.'s (1999) study also showed that verbs are used much less frequently than nouns in academic discourse, and the range of verbs used is quite limited. In particular, so-called *reporting* verbs—*assert, argue, suggest, note,* and so forth—are common and useful for academic writers. However, studies also suggest that verb tense distributions can vary across disciplines, and that this tense variation is not simply a syntactic choice but rather conveys messages about the nature of evidence in that discipline (Conrad, 2008). For instance, in biology, the past tense is used to describe recently completed research, while general statements are made in present tense. History, on the other hand, is primarily focused on events in the past, so the present tense is only rarely used (Conrad, 1996, 2001). A productive exercise for academic writers would thus be to analyze verb tense distributions in excerpts from texts in various disciplines. Similarly, L2 writers should be guided carefully through understanding the formation and appropriate uses of the passive voice, again noting where passives are accepted and frequently used (e.g., scientific and technical writing) and where they are frowned on (humanities and legal writing).

While analysis and understanding of how nouns and verbs are used in academic writing is fundamental and valuable, the last two items on the chart focus on how lexicogrammatical choices can convey writers' stances and ideas appropriately. In his studies of hedging in academic discourse, Hyland (2008) has discovered that advice given to L2 writers to avoid hedging in order to be "assertive" and "direct" is not always beneficial, as in many disciplines "writers are . . . less certain about their results and have to hedge to protect themselves against being wrong and to show that they respect readers' possible alternative opinions" (p. 74).[13] Not only should L2 writers learn to recognize the purposes of hedging structures, which also include longer phrases/clauses such as *It may be possible* or *It is extremely unlikely*, but again, they need to examine and practice how such hedges function grammatically within sentences. Finally, Conrad (2008) made a helpful distinction between how overt markers of persuasion (modals, conditions, phrases such as *in my opinion*) are used in "everyday argument" such as newspaper editorials but noted that they are far less common in academic writing, where writers' arguments are expressed through statements of fact in simple present or past tense, followed by presentations of evidence to support these straightforward statements (see pp. 118–121). Conrad also highlighted "stance bundles" (pp. 124–125), phrases that convey the writer's attitude toward a topic or a specific assertion within that topic, such as *it is important to* or *studies have shown that*. There is some overlap between Conrad's discussion of stance bundles and Hyland's description of hedges, but the notion of stance bundles is broader in scope.

The categories shown in Figure 6.6 can give writing instructors a useful head start in identifying syntactic constructions that could be useful for their students to observe and to practice. Indeed, effective coverage of the six categories shown there could easily consume any and all time that writing instructors may be able to devote to this type of language development. However, it is important that teachers use their own judgment about student needs to identify lexical and grammatical features to present. These needs are defined by a combination of student ability level (in the L2 and especially L2 writing), which also includes their formal knowledge of terms and rules that can help them to grasp the uses of these structures, of features illustrated in texts students are reading, and of tasks they will need to accomplish in writing. At minimum, teachers need to help students appreciate cross-disciplinary and cross-genre distinctions and to perform their own analyses of the most relevant features for the written discourses they will be reading and producing.

The recommended general methods for presenting these syntactic features are similar to those discussed earlier in the chapter and in Chapter 5. Teachers should (1) use authentic texts to help students observe the natural occurrences of targeted syntactic features; (2) design mini-lessons to help students learn the rules behind the uses of those features; and (3) give students repeated opportunities to apply their knowledge to texts they are writing or have already written. It is important that such bottom-up linguistic work be carefully contextualized within the larger goals of the writing course or it may not achieve its desired effects (improved language control and stronger writing).

Using Corpus Findings and Methods for Writing Instruction

As already noted earlier in this book, corpus research—even just reading it, let alone actually conducting it—can seem intimidating to many writing instructors, depending on their interests and backgrounds, as it requires both a strong background in formal linguistics as well as familiarity with advanced statistical techniques (Conrad, 2005, 2008; Ferris, 2011). Recognizing this, some corpus linguists have turned their attention to producing classroom materials based on corpus findings and how-to resources for teachers. Space does not permit exhaustive coverage of this topic here, but readers are encouraged to consult two recent books for practical and detailed information and suggestions (Bennett, 2010; Reppen, 2010).[14]

Corpus-Informed Resources

Materials based on corpus linguistics research have proliferated over the past 10 to 15 years. They fall into three major categories: (1) reference materials for teachers; (2) reference materials for students; and (3) textbooks for student use. In the first category, the most important reference materials are the corpus-based reference grammars by Biber et al. (1999) and Carter and McCarthy (2006). Both of these works provide detailed, empirically verified information about lexical and syntactic patterns in spoken and written English, and teachers can consult them for ideas about structures to present in the classroom. If one or both of these volumes is out of the financial reach of an individual teacher, it may be possible for a program or campus library to obtain it. Writing instructors interested in English for Academic Purposes may also wish to consult Biber's (2006) book, *University English*, which highlights not only the language found in academic texts but in other types of written university discourse (e.g., catalogs, course descriptions, etc.). For more detailed discussions of vocabulary research in particular, readers might look at work by Nation (2001), Schmitt (2010), and Coxhead (2000). These resources offer empirically grounded information for teachers about language forms, how they work, and how they co-occur with other forms. Previous generations of reference and classroom materials were often based on materials developers' best guesses about structures that needed to be covered in language courses, and as noted by Conrad (2008), "Although we 'know' a lot, we aren't always conscious of how language is used, and sometimes our intuitions or anecdotal evidence are misleading" (p. 126). In contrast, corpus-based reference materials can move practitioners beyond simple intuitions or anecdotes.

A second important category of corpus-informed materials are learner dictionaries, and they include the *Cambridge Dictionary of American English* (Cassidy, 2007), *Cambridge Academic Content Dictionary* (2008), and the *Longman Dictionary of Contemporary English* (2010). Classroom activities based on learner dictionaries may include work on individual vocabulary items or analysis of collocations and other lexicogrammatical information. Students can be guided through using dictionaries to research structures they are curious about from their reading and/or items they might like to use in their writing; this work could also be incorporated at the editing phase, where students are asked to take a current draft, identify a few words or structures they are not sure about, and use the dictionary to analyze whether they believe they have used the items appropriately. The most important benefit of such activities for a writing class is familiarizing students with the resources so that they can use them independently.

Classroom textbooks based on corpus research findings are a fairly recent but rapidly growing segment of the materials market. Bennett (2010, pp. 28–29; see also Reppen, 2010) provided an up-to-date summary of such classroom materials from various publishers; some of the most notable include the *Touchstone* integrated skills series (McCarthy, McCarten, & Sandiford, 2005; see also McCarthy, 2004) and several texts based on the Academic Word List (Huntley, 2006; Schmitt & Schmitt, 2005). The Cengage Heinle *English for Academic Success* series includes four-level integrated sets of reading, writing, and vocabulary texts that are corpus-informed. While teachers may or may not wish to adopt such texts for their own writing courses—textbook selection should, of course, be based on a wide range of criteria (see Ferris & Hedgcock, 2005; Hedgcock & Ferris, 2009)—these classroom materials can give them ideas about types of corpus-informed activities and exercises that might be useful for their particular students.

Corpora in the Classroom

The previous section focused on research-based resources developed for teachers and students by corpus linguists. However, some corpus researchers encourage teachers to go a step further by conducting their own corpus studies or even training their students to do so (Bennett, 2010; Conrad, 2008; O'Keefe, McCarthy, & Carter, 2007; Reppen, 2010). Such "studies" could be as simple as using concordances such as those provided in the *Compleat Lexical Tutor* to analyze vocabulary use in a professional or student text; even students can be guided to do so in class or for homework. The recent books by Bennett (2010) and Reppen (2010) both describe the various corpora and text analysis programs available online for free and provide suggestions as to how teachers can use them to develop classroom materials. Bennett (2010) also provides a very useful step-by-step description of how teachers can use a free program called TextSTAT to compile and analyze a corpus of student writing for errors. Both Bennett and Reppen include varied field-tested ideas for integrating corpus work into classroom instruction in ways that complement other activity types.

It should be easy to gather from this section that corpus linguistics research is a thriving and productive area of applied linguistics; indeed, it has been so for well over 20 years now. Corpus-informed reference and classroom materials and how-to resources for teachers, most of which have appeared within the past decade, are a welcome addition to the field. Trying to describe the vast range of resources in a short section of a single chapter reminds me of my experience with reading *Estate Planning for Dummies* (Caverly & Simon, 2003) a few years ago. After reading the entire book, I was left with a crucial take-away: This field is too complex and it changes too rapidly to be covered adequately within a short space—consult an expert (i.e., an estate-planning attorney). Readers interested in learning more about corpus linguistics research and its applications for the teaching of writing are strongly encouraged to consult the more extensive and teacher-friendly resources I have already cited, especially the books by Bennett (2010), Reppen (2010), and the collection by Reid (2008, Ch. 1–4; 6).

Concluding Thoughts

The ideas in this chapter begin with two assumptions: (1) ongoing language development is an important concern for teachers of L2 writers and (2) intensive language analysis can and should be productively integrated into a writing course syllabus along with the various other types of activities that a typical class might include. The Postscript that ends this book addresses syllabus design issues a bit further. The key point to reiterate here is that such "bottom-up" language analysis should flow naturally from reading and/or writing tasks the class is already doing, rather than as stand-alone, isolated activities.

Nonetheless, teachers may find the concepts here a bit daunting. Philosophically, they may wonder if an intensive focus on bits of language such as vocabulary and collocations is really consistent with developing students' writing processes and teaching them to think analytically and critically. Practically, they may be concerned that (a) they themselves do not have a strong enough linguistics background to be able to approach such instruction and (b) they will not be able to fit language development emphases into an already crowded course syllabus. We have tried to demystify "academic language development" in this chapter by focusing on four specific subtopics:

1. the ways in which teachers can maximize intensive and extensive reading activities to help students' ongoing L2 acquisition
2. specific ideas surrounding the teaching of vocabulary and vocabulary analysis strategies
3. research-based suggestions about grammatical structures that may be important for academic writers to attend to and master
4. resources from corpus linguistics research that can help teachers address the previous three subtopics more systematically and confidently.

This was a challenging chapter to write because there is simply *so much* information to try to convey (and I have barely scratched the surface). However, I am convinced that teachers of L2 writers in particular must go beyond top-down higher-order concerns and even beyond the treatment of error in their students' texts. L2 writers are simultaneously learning to compose and acquiring more proficient control of the L2 itself. This is a task of great difficulty and complexity, one that advanced writers of their own primary language (i.e., many teachers of L2 writers) tend to underestimate. Writing teachers tend to do a better job with the first half of the task—teaching students to compose—than they do with the second part, helping students develop the linguistic repertoire they will need to complete their writing tasks successfully. While I am well aware that this chapter has barely begun to explore such a large and important topic, I do hope that it has heightened readers' awareness and curiosity about it.

Questions for Discussion and Application

1. This chapter argues that "bottom-up" instruction on vocabulary and grammar could be a valuable addition to a writing course. Are you intrigued by this idea, intimidated by it, or resistant to it? Why?

2. Have you used extensive reading as part of a writing course you have taught? Would you consider doing so? What do you think of the points raised in this chapter about how extensive reading can facilitate students' ongoing language development?

3. As described in this chapter, Folse (2008) specifically recommends that teachers incorporate a program of vocabulary instruction into their writing courses. What is your reaction to this suggestion?

4. The issue of plagiarism or textual borrowing was also raised in the section on vocabulary. What is your reaction to the point (raised by Folse and discussed further here) that what teachers might consider "plagiarism" can really be diagnosed as "inadequate vocabulary and paraphrasing skills"? Do you buy that argument, or that is simply letting students off too easily?

5. Figure 6.6 provides a list of some (lexico)grammatical emphases that could be productively incorporated into a writing class. Thinking about classes you have taught or might teach, which one(s) could you see yourself presenting? Are there others you might add to the list?

6. Which type(s) of corpus-informed resources (teacher reference materials, dictionaries or textbooks for students, actual corpora) have you used in the classroom or could you see yourself potentially using? If the answer is none, why not?

Further Reading

These sources will help you go further in understanding the major themes developed in this chapter. Complete bibliographic information is provided in the References section at the end of the book. The list is presented alphabetically rather than chronologically or thematically.

Bennett, G. (2010).
Byrd, P., & Bunting, J. (2008).
Conrad, S. (2008).
Cortes, V. (2004).
Coxhead, A. (2000).
Folse, K. (2008).
Hedgcock, J., & Ferris, D. (2009).
Hyland, K. (2008).
Reppen, R. (2010).
Schuemann, C. (2008).

CHAPTER 6 NOTES

1. See Hedgcock & Ferris, 2009; Hudson, 2007; Koda, 2004; Nation, 2001.

2. For background on the corpus-based Academic Word List, see Coxhead (2000, 2006); and Coxhead & Byrd (2007).

3. Examples of other syntactic choices are discussed later in the chapter. See also Bennett (2010); Biber (2006); Byrd & Bunting (2008); Conrad (2008); Hinkel (2004); Reppen (2010); and Zwier & Bennett (2006).

4. See, for example, Garner (2001) and Wydick (2005).

5. See www.standards-schmandards.com/exhibits/rix/.

6. For more discussion of intensive reading activities, see Hedgcock & Ferris (2009) and Seymour & Walsh (2006).

7. See Aebersold & Field (1997); Day & Bamford (1998); Hedgcock & Ferris (2009); and Krashen (2004).

8. See Folse, 2008, for a cogent review of this research.

9. The AWL Highlighter is available at www.nottingham.ac.uk/~alzsh3/acvocab/awlhighlighter.htm.

10. For example, if the student/teacher designates "Level 5," all AWL words from Levels 1–5 will be highlighted within the text, but the words from Levels 6–10 will not be.

11. See, for example, research reported by Biber (1988; 2006); Biber, Conrad, & Cortes (2004); Biber et al. (1999); Carter & McCarthy (2006); Cortes (2004); and Nation (2001). For further discussion of lexical bundles and their classroom utility, see Bennett (2010); Byrd & Bunting (2008); Conrad (2008); Coxhead & Byrd (2007); and Reppen (2010).

12. The suffixes are *–tion, -ity, -er, -ness, -ism,* and *–ment* (Biber et al., 1999; Reppen, 2010, p. 23).

13. The most frequently used hedges in academic writing are *assume, could, indicate, likely, may, might, possible(ly), seem, suggest,* and *would* (Hyland, 2008, p. 71).

14. For very accessible and useful introductory material aimed specifically at the teaching of L2 writing, readers may also wish to consult several chapters (Byrd & Bunting, Conrad, Folse, Hyland, and Schuemann) in the edited collection *Writing Myths* (Reid, 2008).

Postscript:
Summary and Putting It All Together

Throughout this book, we have argued that error treatment and the even larger concern of facilitating L2 student writers' ongoing language development are critical issues for teachers of L2 writers. Some composition instructors may be uncomfortable with this stance, saying as did one recent reviewer of another project I was working on, "I don't teach grammar and I don't *want* to teach grammar."[1] This book is designed for instructors who *do* want to have a better understanding of the specific language issues facing their students, especially L2 writers, of what the research suggests about ways to best help them, and of specific practical steps they can take to sharpen their own language-focused feedback and classroom instruction.

Looking at all of these components in isolation might be a bit overwhelming for writing teachers, who wonder how they can possibly afford the class time to incorporate all of these error treatment components. The solution to this is to build error treatment and language development as a regular, cyclical part of the writing process in the classroom. Teachers might find this before-during-after sequence helpful in envisioning how they can integrate language development/error treatment into a writing course syllabus.

Language Development Sequence for Writing Teachers

Before Teaching the Course

- If this is your first time teaching this course at this institution, ask other teachers or administrators for background information and advice about the language levels of the students and things they might need assistance with. Also find out if you can examine any student writing samples or if there are texts, online sources, or campus resources that other teachers have found helpful for teaching this class.

- If you have taught this same course before, do some reflection: What went well? What did students struggle with? What were characteristics of the texts of stronger and weaker writers? Look back at your syllabus and daily lesson materials: Is there anything that didn't go as well as you hoped (or went very well)? What can you learn from this reflection to help you plan your next course?

- As you select texts and plan writing tasks for your course, make a list of vocabulary and syntactic structures that might be (a) challenging for this class and (b) elicited/required for success on the writing assignments.

- When you write your syllabus, leave space at appropriate intervals for editing workshops, common error mini-lessons, and language analysis workshops. You may or may not want to be more specific about topics for those workshops or mini-lessons until you have assessed your new class, but the spaces on the syllabus ensure that you will include them. These should not be inserted randomly but rather integrated naturally with other reading and writing tasks also being completed.

- Also leave space on your syllabus for multiple-drafting, revision, and editing activities, and for points in the writing process where you will provide written or oral feedback, and be sure to allow enough turn-around time to do the job effectively.

- Consider how language development will be part of your assessment and grading scheme. For example, how does it factor into grading rubrics for individual papers or a final portfolio? Will you consider errors and language use differently in timed writing tasks? Will you assign students homework or class exercises in which they edit and analyze their own errors? Will you give vocabulary or grammar quizzes? Will you incorporate extensive reading or student-directed vocabulary learning (e.g., by assigning a vocabulary notebook or cards)?

- Research other resources outside of your course that may be helpful for you in your own teaching and/or for student self-study. These might include some of the corpus-informed materials discussed in Chapter 6, online writing labs that provide mini-lessons and practice exercises for grammar/usage topics, and campus writing centers or tutoring services (find out if they have an explicit policy or philosophy against helping student writers with language issues).

During the Course

- Gather detailed information about your students as soon as possible: background questionnaires that give you a snapshot of the types of prior educational experiences they may have had, error analyses based on a diagnostic writing sample the first day or week of class, or grammar knowledge pre-tests or questionnaires that help you assess their formal understanding of grammar (see Chapters 4 and 5 for more detail on these processes).

- Give a mini-lesson early in the course about editing and proofreading strategies (see Chapter 5).

- Provide appropriate written and oral feedback at key stages of the writing process (see Chapter 4).
- Provide in-class opportunities for students to do peer- and self-editing activities (Chapter 5).
- Require students to revise/edit, reflect on, and analyze/ chart their common writing errors after receiving teacher or peer feedback (Chapter 5).
- After responding to a set of student papers, deliver mini-lessons involving problems common to most of the class and/or provide resources for smaller groups of students or individuals so that they can do further study on common errors (Chapter 5).
- In conjunction with reading activities and at the final stages of writing tasks, deliver mini-lessons on key vocabulary and syntactic structures that you have (a) identified as being relevant to your other course materials (reading and writing assignments) and (b) identified as being areas of potential weakness for some or most of your students (Chapter 6).
- As you respond to and assess student writing and other graded activities (error logs or analyses, quizzes, vocabulary notebooks, etc.), place the *appropriate* emphasis—not too much, not too little—on word- and sentence-level accuracy and expression. Do not ignore it and do not obsess about it.

After Teaching the Course

- Reflect on and make detailed notes about how things went: What went well? What would you like to improve on the next time you teach this course or one like it? Part of this evaluation should include how your students did in improving their overall writing, especially in reducing their error frequencies, utilizing effective editing strategies, and developing more effective lexical and syntactic control and style in their writing.

- Consider what you could do to be better prepared for language development and error treatment the next time you teach, and commit to taking at least one step forward in your own professional development. For example, you might read some of the studies cited in Chapters 1 and 2, take some of the practical steps described in Chapter 3, or investigate some of the recent corpus materials discussed in Chapter 6.

Finally, you may wish to articulate and revisit your own evolving philosophies and opinions on language development and treatment of error. Before reading this book, which statement(s) most closely resembled your thinking?

1. I haven't thought much about how to teach grammar, mark errors, and develop language awareness in a writing class.
2. I learned in my teacher preparation program that errors are unimportant and that grammar teaching is ineffective, so I am uncomfortable with the notion of focusing extensively on errors and language in the teaching of writing.
3. I know that L2 writers have language errors that need to be addressed, but I am not sure of the best ways to go about this. I am also not sure that I myself have the language background needed to approach this concern.
4. I know that error treatment is important, and I have some strategies that I think have worked for me and my students, but I'm also aware that there is a lot of new research out there about corrective feedback, genre knowledge, and corpus linguistics, and I have the feeling I'm missing a few things and could tune up my skills.

Has reading this book influenced your thinking about your own philosophy? Does reflecting on your own past and current teaching of L2 writers inform your opinion? It could be helpful to write a sentence or two that states your philosophy and review it after teaching a few more courses. Do your practices match your stated beliefs?

Concluding Thoughts

Preparing oneself to treat student error (see Chapter 3) and carrying out a comprehensive error treatment and language development plan (Chapters 4–6) is challenging and demanding for teachers of L2 writers. While no one would argue that all of teachers' time and attention should be consumed with dealing with student errors, this concern is definitely one that teachers must indeed take seriously. In many contexts, students' success or failure in their academic endeavors or their future careers may hinge in a large part on their ability to improve the accuracy and clarity of their written work. With few exceptions, it is unlikely that they will be able to achieve the high levels of accuracy demanded and expected without teacher intervention and training. While it may be tempting to simply ignore the need for error treatment, for most L2 writing teachers, to do so would be to ill-serve our students.

POSTSCRIPT NOTE

1. I am guessing, however, that such teachers have not made it all the way to the postscript of this particular book!

References

Aebersold, J., & Field, M. (1997). *From reader to reading teacher: Issues and strategies for second language classrooms.* Cambridge, U.K.: Cambridge University Press.

Anson, C.M. (2000). Response and the social construction of error. *Assessing Writing, 7,* 5–21.

Ascher, A. (1993). *Think about editing.* Boston: Heinle.

Ashwell, T. (2000). Patterns of teacher response to student writing in a multiple-draft composition classroom: Is content feedback followed by form feedback the best method? *Journal of Second Language Writing, 9,* 227–258.

Barry, A.K. (2002). *English grammar: Language as human behavior* (2nd Ed.). Englewood Cliffs, NJ: Prentice-Hall.

Bates, L., Lane, J., & Lange, E. (1993). *Writing clearly: Responding to student writing.* Boston: Heinle.

Beason, L. (2001). Ethos and error: How business people react to errors. *College Composition and Communication, 53,* 33–64.

Bennett, G. (2010). *Using corpora in the language learning classroom.* Ann Arbor: University of Michigan Press.

Biber, D. (1988). *Variation across speech and writing.* Cambridge, U.K.: Cambridge University Press.

Biber, D. (2006). *University English: A corpus-based study of written and spoken registers.* Amsterdam: John Benjamins.

Biber, D., Conrad, S., & Cortes, V. (2004). *If you look at . . . :* Lexical bundles in university teaching and textbooks. *Applied Linguistics, 25,* 371–405.

Biber, D., Conrad, S., Reppen, R., Byrd, P., & Helt, M. (2002). Speaking and writing in the university: A multi-dimensional comparison. *TESOL Quarterly, 36,* 9–48.

Biber, D., Johansson, C., Leech, S., Conrad, S., & Finegan, E. (1999). *The Longman grammar of spoken and written English.* London: Longman.

Bitchener, J. (2008). Evidence in support of written corrective feedback. *Journal of Second Language Writing, 17,* 102–118.

Bitchener, J., & Ferris, D. (2012). *Written corrective feedback in second language acquisition and writing.* New York: Routledge/Taylor & Francis.

Bitchener, J., & Knoch, U. (2008). The value of written corrective feedback for migrant and international students. *Language Teaching Research, 12,* 409–431.

Bitchener, J., & Knoch, U. (2009). The value of a focused approach to written corrective feedback. *ELT Journal, 63,* 204–211.

Bitchener, J., & Knoch, U. (2010a). The contribution of written corrective feedback to language development: A ten-month investigation. *Applied Linguistics, 31,* 193–214.

Bitchener, J., & Knoch, U. (2010b). Raising the linguistic accuracy level of advanced L2 writers with written corrective feedback. *Journal of Second Language Writing, 19,* 207–217.

Bitchener, J., Young, S., & Cameron, D. (2005). The effect of different types of corrective feedback on ESL student writing. *Journal of Second Language Writing, 9,* 227–258.

Bosher, S., & Rowecamp, J. (1998). The refugee/immigrant in higher education: The role of educational background. *College ESL, 8* (1), 23–42.

Brannon, L., & Knoblauch, C.H. (1982). On students' rights to their own texts: A model of teacher response. *College Composition and Communication, 33,* 157–166.

Brown, D. (2010, March). *Reshaping the value of grammatical feedback on L2 writing using colors.* Paper presented at the International TESOL Convention, Boston, MA.

Brown, H.D. (2007). *Principles of language learning and teaching* (5th Ed.). White Plains, NY: Pearson Education.

Bruton, A. (2009). Improving accuracy is not the only reason for writing, and even if it were . . . . *System, 37,* 600–613.

Burt, M.K., & Kiparsky, C. (1972). *The gooficon: A repair manual for English.* Rowley, MA: Newbury House.

Byrd, P., & Bunting, J. (2008). Myth 3: Where grammar is concerned, one size fits all. In J. Reid (Ed.), *Writing myths: Applying second language research to classroom teaching* (pp. 42–69). Ann Arbor: University of Michigan Press.

Byrd, P., & Reid, J.M. (1998). *Grammar in the composition classroom: Essays on teaching ESL for college-bound students.* Boston: Heinle.

Cambridge Academic Content Dictionary (2008). Cambridge, U.K.: Cambridge University Press.

Carson, J. G., & Nelson, G. L. (1994). Writing groups: Cross-cultural issues. *Journal of Second Language Writing, 3*(1): 17–30.

Carter, R., & McCarthy, M. (2006). *Cambridge grammar of English: A comprehensive guide. Spoken and written English grammar and usage.* Cambridge, U.K.: Cambridge University Press.

Cassidy, C.-J. (2007). *Cambridge Dictionary of American English* (2nd Ed.). Cambridge, U.K.: Cambridge University Press.

Caverly, B., & Simon, J. (2003). *Estate planning for dummies.* New York: Wiley.

Celce-Murcia, M., & Larsen-Freeman, D. (1998). *The grammar book: An ESL/EFL teacher's course* (2nd Ed.). Boston: Heinle.

Chandler, J. (2003). The efficacy of various kinds of error feedback for improvement in the accuracy and fluency of L2 student writing. *Journal of Second Language Writing, 12,* 267–296.

Chaney, S.J. (1999). *The effect of error types on error correction and revision.* California State University, Sacramento, Department of English, M.A. thesis.

Cohen, A. (1987). Student processing of feedback on their compositions. In A.L. Wenden & J. Rubin (Eds.), *Learner strategies in language learning* (pp. 57–69). Englewood Cliffs, NJ: Prentice-Hall.

Cohen, A., & Cavalcanti, M. (1990). Feedback on written compositions: Teacher and student verbal reports. In B. Kroll (Ed.), *Second language writing: Research insights for the classroom* (pp. 155–177). Cambridge, U.K.: Cambridge University Press.

Cohen, A.D., & Robbins, M. (1976). Toward assessing interlanguage performance: The relationship between selected errors, learners' characteristics, and learners' expectations. *Language Learning, 26,* 45–66.

Collier, V. P. (1987). Age and rate of acquisition of second language for academic purposes. *TESOL Quarterly, 21,* 617–641.

Collier, V. P. (1989). How long? A synthesis of research on academic achievement in a second language. *TESOL Quarterly, 23,* 509–531.

Conference on College Composition and Communication (CCCC) (2009). Statement on second language writing and writers. www.ncte.org/cccc/resources/positions/secondlangwriting

Connor, U. (1996). *Contrastive rhetoric: Cross-cultural aspects of second-language writing.* Cambridge, U.K.: Cambridge University Press.

Connor, U., & Kaplan, R.B. (Eds.) (1987). *Writing across languages: Analysis of L2 text.* Rowley, MA: Newbury House.

Connors, R., & Lunsford, A.A. (1988). Frequency of formal errors in current college writing, or Ma and Pa Kettle do research. *College Composition and Communication, 39*(4), 395–409.

Conrad, S.M. (1996). Investigating academic texts with corpus-based techniques: An example from biology. *Linguistics and Education, 8,* 299–326.

Conrad, S.M. (2001). Variation among disciplinary texts: A comparison of textbooks and journal articles in biology and history. In S. Conrad & D. Biber (Eds.), *Multi-dimensional studies of register variation in English* (pp. 94–107). Harlow, U.K.: Pearson Education.

Conrad, S.M. (2005). Corpus linguistics and L2 teaching. In E. Hinkel (Ed.), *Handbook of research in second language teaching and learning* (pp. 393–409). Mahwah, NJ: Lawrence Erlbaum.

Conrad, S.M. (2008). Myth 6: Corpus-based research is too complicated to be useful for writing teachers. In J. Reid (Ed.), *Writing myths: Applying second language research to classroom teaching* (pp. 115–139). Ann Arbor: University of Michigan Press.

Corder, S.P. (1967). The significance of learners' errors . *International Review of Applied Linguistics, 5,* 161–170.

Cortes, V. (2004). Lexical bundles in published and student disciplinary writing: Examples from history and biology. *English for Specific Purposes, 23,* 397–423.

Coxhead, A. (2000). A new academic word list. *TESOL Quarterly, 34*(2), 213–238.

Coxhead, A. (2006). *Essentials of teaching academic vocabulary.* Boston: Houghton Mifflin.

Coxhead, A., & Byrd, P. (2007). Preparing writing teachers to teach the vocabulary and grammar of academic prose. *Journal of Second Language Writing, 16*(3), 129–147.

Crusan, D. (2010). *Assessment in the second language writing classroom.* Ann Arbor: University of Michigan Press.

Davis, C. (1997). A Mason-Dixon memory. In J. Canfield, M. V. Hanson, H. McCarty, & M. McCarty (Eds.), *A 4th course of chicken soup for the soul* (pp. 23–29). Deerfield Beach, FL: Health Communications, Inc.

Day, R. R., & Bamford, J. (1998). *Extensive reading in the second language classroom.* Cambridge, U.K.: Cambridge University Press.

Doughty, C., & Williams, J. (Eds.) (1998). *Focus on form in classroom second language acquisition.* Cambridge, U.K.: Cambridge University Press.

Eckman, F. (1977). Markedness and the contrastive analysis hypothesis. *Language Learning, 27,* 315–330.

Elbow, P. (1973). *Writing without teachers.* Oxford, U.K.: Oxford University Press.

Ellis, R., Sheen, Y., Murakami, M., & Takashima, H. (2008). The effects of focused and unfocused written corrective feedback in an English as a foreign language context. *System, 36,* 353–371.

Enginarlar, H. (1993). Student response to teacher feedback in EFL writing. *System, 21,* 193–204.

Eskey, D.E. (1983). Meanwhile, back in the real world . . . . Accuracy and fluency in second language teaching. *TESOL Quarterly, 17,* 315–323.

Evans, N., Hartshorn, J., McCollum, R., & Wolfersberger, M. (2010). Contextualizing corrective feedback in second language writing pedagogy. *Language Teaching Research, 14,* 445–464.

Ewert, D. (2009). L2 writing conferences: Investigating teacher talk. *Journal of Second Language Writing, 18,* 251–269.

Fathman, A., & Whalley, E. (1990). Teacher response to student writing: Focus on form versus content. In B. Kroll (Ed.), *Second language writing: Research insights for the classroom* (pp. 178–190). Cambridge, U.K.: Cambridge University Press.

Ferris, D.R. (1995a). Can advanced ESL students be taught to correct their most serious and frequent errors? *CATESOL Journal, 8(1),* 41–62.

Ferris, D.R. (1995b). Student reactions to teacher response in multiple-draft composition classrooms, *TESOL Quarterly, 29,* 33–53.

Ferris, D.R. (1995c). Teaching students to self-edit. *TESOL Journal 4(4),* 18–22.

Ferris, D.R. (1997). The influence of teacher commentary on student revision. *TESOL Quarterly, 31,* 315–339.

Ferris, D.R. (1999a). The case for grammar correction in L2 writing classes: A response to Truscott (1996). *Journal of Second Language Writing, 8,* 1–10.

Ferris, D.R. (1999b). One size does not fit all: Response and revision issues for immigrant student writers. In L. Harklau, K. Losey, & M. Siegal (Eds.), *Generation 1.5 meets college composition* (pp. 143–157). Mahwah, NJ: Lawrence Erlbaum.

Ferris, D.R. (2002). *Treatment of error in second language student writing.* Ann Arbor: University of Michigan Press.

Ferris, D.R. (2003). *Response to student writing: Research implications for second language students.* Mahwah, NJ: Lawrence Erlbaum.

Ferris, D.R. (2004). The "grammar correction" debate in L2 writing: Where are we, and where do we go from here? (and what do we do in the meantime...?) *Journal of Second Language Writing, 13,* 49–62.

Ferris, D.R. (2006). Does error feedback help student writers? New evidence on the short- and long-term effects of written error correction. In K. Hyland & F. Hyland (Eds.), *Feedback in second language writing: Contexts and issues* (pp. 81–104). Cambridge, U.K.: Cambridge University Press.

Ferris, D.R. (2008). Myth 5: Students must learn to correct all their writing errors. In J. Reid (Ed.), *Writing myths: Applying second language research to classroom teaching* (pp. 90–114). Ann Arbor: University of Michigan Press.

Ferris, D.R. (2009). *Teaching college writing to diverse student populations.* Ann Arbor: University of Michigan Press.

Ferris, D.R. (2010). Second language writing research and written corrective feedback in SLA: Intersections and practical applications. *Studies in Second Language Acquisition, 32,* 181–201.

Ferris, D.R. (2011). Written discourse analysis and L2 teaching. In E. Hinkel (Ed.), *Handbook of research in second language teaching and learning,* Vol. II (pp. 643–662). New York: Routledge.

Ferris, D.R., Brown, J., Liu, H., & Stine, M.E.A. (2011). Responding to L2 writers in college writing classes: What teachers say and what they do. *TESOL Quarterly, 45,* 207–234.

Ferris, D., & Hedgcock, J.S. (2005). *Teaching ESL composition: Purpose, process, & practice* (2nd Ed.). Mahwah, NJ: Lawrence Erlbaum.

Ferris, D.R., Liu, H., & Rabie, B. (2011). "The job of teaching writing": Teacher views of responding to student writing. *Writing and Pedagogy, 3,* 39–77.

Ferris, D.R., Liu, H., Senna, M., & Sinha, A. (2010, April). *Written corrective feedback & individual variation in L2 writing.* Paper presented at the CATESOL State Conference, Santa Clara, CA.

Ferris, D.R., Liu, H., Senna, M., & Sinha, A. (2011, March). *Written corrective feedback & individual differences: A tale of two student writers.* Paper presented at AAAL Conference, Chicago, IL.

Ferris, D.R., & Roberts, B.J. (2001). Error feedback in L2 writing classes: How explicit does it need to be? *Journal of Second Language Writing, 10,* 161–184.

Foin, A., & Lange, E. (2007). Generation 1.5 writers' success in correcting errors marked on an out-of-class paper. *CATESOL Journal, 19,* 146–163.

Folse, K.S. (2004). *Vocabulary myths: Applying second language research to classroom teaching*. Ann Arbor: University of Michigan Press.

Folse, K.S. (2008). Myth 1: Teaching vocabulary is not the writing teacher's job. In J. Reid (Ed.) *Writing myths: Applying second language research to classroom teaching* (pp. 1–17). Ann Arbor: University of Michigan Press.

Folse, K. (2009). *Keys to teaching grammar to English language learners: A practical handbook*. Ann Arbor: University of Michigan Press.

Folse, K., Solomon, E., & Smith-Palinkas, B. (2003). *Top 20: Great grammar for great writing*. Boston: Heinle.

Fox, L. (1992). *Focus on editing*. London: Longman.

Frantzen, D. (1995). The effects of grammar supplementation on written accuracy in an intermediate Spanish content course. *Modern Language Journal, 79,* 329–344.

Frantzen, D., & Rissel, D. (1987). Learner self-correction of written compositions: What does it show us? In B. VanPatten, T.R. Dvorak, & J.F. Lee (Eds.), *Foreign language learning: A research perspective* (pp. 92–107). Cambridge, MA: Newbury House.

Frodesen, J. (1991). Grammar in writing. In M. Celce-Murcia (Ed.), *Teaching English as a second or foreign language* (2nd ed.) (pp. 264–276). Boston: Heinle.

Frodesen, J., & Holten, C. (2003). Grammar and the ESL writing class. In B. Kroll (Ed.), *Exploring the dynamics of second language writing* (pp. 141–161). Cambridge, U.K.: Cambridge University Press.

Garner, B.A. (2001). *Legal writing in plain English*. Chicago: University of Chicago Press.

Goldstein, L., & Conrad, S. (1990). Student input and the negotiation of meaning in ESL writing conferences. *TESOL Quarterly, 24,* 443–460.

Gray-Rosendale, L. (1998). Inessential writings: Shaughnessy's legacy in a socially constructed landscape. *Journal of Basic Writing, 17*(3), 43–75.

Guénette, D. (2007). Is feedback pedagogically correct?: Research design issues in studies of feedback on writing. *Journal of Second Language Writing, 16,* 40–53.

Hairston, M. (1981). Not all errors are created equal: Nonacademic readers in the professions respond to lapses in usage. *College English, 43,* 794–806.

Harklau, L. (2000). From the "good kids" to the "worst": Representations of English language learners across educational settings. *TESOL Quarterly, 34,* 35–67.

Harklau, L., Losey, K., & Siegal, M. (Eds.) (1999). *Generation 1.5 meets college composition: Issues in the teaching of writing to U.S.-educated learners of ESL.* Mahwah, NJ: Lawrence Erlbaum.

Harklau, L., & Siegal, M. (2009). Immigrant youth and higher education: An overview. In M. Roberge, M. Siegal, & L. Harklau (Eds.), *Generation 1.5 in college composition* (pp. 25–34). New York: Routledge.

Hartshorn, J.K., Evans, N.W., Merrill, P.F., Sudweeks, R.R., Strong-Krause, D., & Anderson, N.J. (2010). The effects of dynamic corrective feedback on ESL writing accuracy. *TESOL Quarterly, 44,* 84–109.

Hartwell, P. (1985). Grammar, grammars, and the teaching of grammar. *College English, 47,* 105–127.

Haswell, R.H. (1983). Minimal marking. *College English, 45,* 600–604.

Hedgcock, J.S., & Ferris, D.R. (2009). *Teaching readers of English: Students, texts, and contexts.* New York: Routledge.

Hedgcock, J., & Lefkowitz, N. (1994). Feedback on feedback: Assessing learner receptivity in second language writing. *Journal of Second Language Writing, 3,* 141–163.

Hedgcock, J., & Lefkowitz, N. (1996). Some input on input: Two analyses of student response to expert feedback on L2 writing. *Modern Language Journal, 80,* 287–308.

Hendrickson, J.M. (1978). Error correction in foreign language teaching: Recent theory, research, and practice. *Modern Language Journal, 62,* 387–398.

Hendrickson, J.M. (1980). The treatment of error in written work. *Modern Language Journal, 64,* 216–221.

Higgs, T., & Clifford, R. (1982). The push toward communication. In T. Higgs (Ed.), *Curriculum, competence, and the foreign language teacher* (pp. 57–79). Skokie, IL: National Textbook Company.

Hinkel, E. (2004). *Teaching academic ESL writing: Practical techniques in vocabulary and grammar.* Mahwah, NJ: Lawrence Erlbaum.

Hirvela, A. (2004). *Connecting reading and writing in second language writing instruction.* Ann Arbor: University of Michigan Press.

Horowitz, D. (1986). Process not product: Less than meets the eye. *TESOL Quarterly, 20,* 141–144.

Hudson, T. (2007). *Teaching second language reading.* Oxford, U.K.: Oxford University Press.

Huntley, H. (2006). *Essential academic vocabulary.* Boston: Heinle.

Hyland, K. (1994). Hedging in academic writing and EAP textbooks. *English for Specific Purposes, 13,* 239–256.

Hyland, K. (1998). *Hedging in scientific research articles.* Amsterdam: John Benjamins.

Hyland, K. (2008). Myth 4: Make your academic writing assertive and certain. In J. Reid (Ed.), *Writing myths: Applying second language research to classroom teaching* (pp. 70–89). Ann Arbor: University of Michigan Press.

Hyland, K., & Milton, J. (1997). Hedging in L1 and L2 student writing. *Journal of Second Language Writing, 6,* 183–206.

James, C. (1998). *Errors in language learning and use: Exploring error analysis.* London: Longman.

Janopolous, M. (1992). University faculty tolerance of NS and NNS writing errors. *Journal of Second Language Writing, 1,* 109–122.

Johns, A.M. (1990). L1 composition theories: Implications for developing theories of L2 composition. In B. Kroll (Ed.), *Second language writing: Research insights for the classroom* (pp. 24–36). Cambridge, U.K.: Cambridge University Press.

Johns, A.M. (1995). Genre and pedagogical purposes. *Journal of Second Language Writing, 4,* 181–190.

Johns, A.M. (1997). *Text, role and context: Developing academic literacies.* Cambridge, U.K.: Cambridge University Press.

Johns, A.M. (2003). Genre and ESL/EFL composition instruction. In B. Kroll (Ed.), *Exploring the dynamics of second language writing* (pp. 195–217). Cambridge, U.K.: Cambridge University Press.

Johns, A.M.. (2009). Situated invention and genres: Assisting Generation 1.5 students in developing rhetorical flexibility. In M. Roberge, M. Siegal, & L. Harklau (Eds.), *Generation 1.5 in college composition.* New York: Routledge.

Kaplan, R.B. (1966). Cultural thought patterns in intercultural education. *Language Learning, 16,* 1–20.

Kaplan, R.B. (1987). Cultural thought patterns revisited. In U. Connor & R.B. Kaplan (Eds.), *Writing across languages: Analysis of L2 text* (pp. 9–21). Reading, MA: Addison-Wesley.

Kastorf, J. (1993). Robo teacher. *Sacramento Bee,* May 26, p. F6.

Kepner, C.G. (1991). An experiment in the relationship of types of written feedback to the development of second-language writing skills. *Modern Language Journal, 75,* 305–313.

Koda, K. (2004). *Insights into second language reading: A cross-linguistic approach.* Cambridge, U.K.: Cambridge University Press.

Komura, K. (1999). *Student response to error correction in ESL classrooms.* California State University, Sacramento, Department of English, M.A. thesis.

Krashen, S.D. (1982). *Principles and practices in second language acquisition.* Oxford, U.K.: Pergamon Press.

Krashen, S.D. (1984). *Writing: Research, theory, and application.* Oxford, U.K.: Pergamon Press.

Krashen, S.D. (1985). *Inquiries and insights.* Menlo Park, CA: Alemany Press.

Krashen, S.D. (1988). Do we learn to read by reading? The relationship between free reading and reading ability. In D. Tannen (Ed.), *Linguistics in context: Connecting observation and understanding* (pp. 269–298). Norwood, NJ: Ablex.

Krashen, S.D. (1989). We acquire vocabulary and spelling by reading: Additional evidence for the Input Hypothesis. *Modern Language Journal, 73,* 440–464.

Krashen, S. D. (2004). *The power of reading* (2nd Ed.). Portsmouth, NH: Heinemann.

Lalande, J.F. II (1982). Reducing composition errors: An experiment. *Modern Language Journal, 66,* 140–149.

Lane, J., & Lange, E. (1999). *Writing clearly: An editing guide* (2nd Ed). Boston: Heinle.

Lee, I. (2008). Understanding teachers' written feedback practices in Hong Kong secondary classrooms. *Journal of Second Language Writing, 17* (2), 69–85.

Lee, I. (2009). Ten mismatches between teachers' beliefs and written feedback practice. *ELT Journal, 63* (1), 13–22.

Leki, I. (1990). Coaching from the margins: Issues in written response. In B. Kroll (Ed.), *Second language writing: Research insights for the classroom* (pp. 57–68). Cambridge, U.K.: Cambridge University Press.

Leki, I. (1991). The preferences of ESL students for error correction in college-level writing classes. *Foreign Language Annals, 24,* 203–218.

Leki, I. (1992). *Understanding ESL writers.* Portsmouth, NH: Boynton/Cook Publishers.

Liu, J., & Hansen, J.G. (2002). *Peer response in second language writing classrooms.* Ann Arbor: University of Michigan Press.

Long, M. (1996). The role of linguistic environment in second language acquisition. In W. Ritchie & T. Bhatia (Eds.), *Handbook of second language acquisition* (pp. 413–468). New York: Academic Press.

Longman dictionary of contemporary English (5th Ed.) (2010). White Plains, NY: Pearson Longman.

Lunsford, A.A. (2009). *The everyday writer* (4th Ed.). Boston: Bedford/St. Martin's.

Lunsford, A.A., & Lunsford, K.J. (2008). "Mistakes are a fact of life": A national comparative study. *College Composition and Communication, 59,* 781–806.

Lyster, R.M., & Ranta, L. (1997). Corrective feedback and learner uptake. *Studies in Second Language Acquisition 19,* 37–66.

MacDonald, S.P. (2007). The erasure of language. *College Composition and Communication, 58,* 585–625.

McCarthy, M. (2004). *Touchstone: From corpus to course book.* Cambridge, U.K.: Cambridge University Press.

McCarthy, M., McCarten, J., & Sandiford, H. (2005). *Touchstone.* Cambridge, U.K.: Cambridge University Press.

Matsuda, P.K. (2006). Second language writing in the twentieth century: A situated historical perspective. In P.K. Matsuda, M. Cox, J. Jordan, & C. Ortmeier-Hooper (Eds.), *Second language writing in the composition classroom* (pp. 14–30). Boston: Bedford/St. Martin's.

Matsuda, P. K., & Matsuda, A. (2009). The erasure of resident ESL writers. In M. Roberge, M. Siegal, & L. Harklau (Eds.), *Generation 1.5 in college composition* (pp. 50–64). New York: Routledge.

Montgomery, J.L., & Baker, W. (2007). Teacher-written feedback: Student perceptions, teacher self-assessment, and actual teacher performance. *Journal of Second Language Writing, 16,* 82–99.

Nation, I.S.P. (2001). *Learning vocabulary in another language.* Cambridge, U.K.: Cambridge University Press.

O'Keefe, A., McCarthy, M., & Carter, R. (2007). *From corpus to classroom.* Cambridge, U.K.: Cambridge University Press.

Park, K. (1999). "I really do feel I'm 1.5": The construction of self and community by young Korean Americans. *Amerasia Journal, 25*(1), 139–163.

Patthey-Chavez, G.G., & Ferris, D.R. (1997). Writing conferences and the weaving of multi-voiced texts in college composition. *Research in the Teaching of English, 31,* 51–90.

Polio, C., Fleck, C., & Leder, N. (1998). "If only I had more time": ESL learners' changes in linguistic accuracy on essay revisions. *Journal of Second Language Writing, 7,* 43–68.

Radecki, P., & Swales, J. (1988). ESL student reaction to written comments on their written work. *System, 16,* 355–365.

Raimes, A. (1991). Out of the woods: Emerging traditions in teaching writing. *TESOL Quarterly, 25,* 407–430.

Raimes, A. (2004). *Grammar troublespots.* Cambridge, U.K.: Cambridge University Press.

Reid, J. (1994). Responding to ESL students' texts: The myths of appropriation. *TESOL Quarterly, 28,* 273–292.

Reid, J. (1998a). "Eye" learners and "ear" learners: Identifying the language needs of international students and U.S. resident writers. In P. Byrd & J.M. Reid (Eds.), *Grammar in the composition classroom: Essays on teaching ESL for college-bound students* (pp. 3–17). Boston: Heinle.

Reid, J. (1998b). Responding to ESL student language problems: Error analysis and revision plans. In P. Byrd & J.M. Reid, *Grammar in the composition classroom: Essays on teaching ESL for college-bound students* (pp. 118–137). Boston: Heinle.

Reid, J. (2002). Ask! In L.L. Blanton & B. Kroll (Eds.), *ESL composition tales* (pp. 83–103). Ann Arbor: University of Michigan Press.

Reid, J. (Ed.) (2008). *Writing myths: Applying second language research to classroom teaching.* Ann Arbor: University of Michigan Press.

Rennie, C. (2000). *Error feedback in ESL writing classes: What do students really want?* California State University, Sacramento, Department of English, M.A. thesis.

Reppen, R. (2010). *Using corpora in the language classroom.* Cambridge, U.K.: Cambridge University Press.

Robb, T., Ross, S., & Shortreed, I. (1986). Salience of feedback on error and its effect on EFL writing quality. *TESOL Quarterly, 20,* 83–93.

Roberge, M.M. (2002). California's Generation 1.5 immigrants: What experiences, characteristics, and needs do they bring to our English classes? *CATESOL Journal, 14*(1), 107–129.

Roberge, M., Siegal, M., & Harklau, L. (Eds.) (2009). *Generation 1.5 in college composition.* New York: Routledge.

Roberts, B.J. (1999). *Can error logs raise more than consciousness? The effects of error logs and grammar feedback on ESL students' final drafts.* California State University, Sacramento, Department of English, M.A. thesis.

Sachs, R., & Polio, C. (2007). Learners' uses of two types of written feedback on a L2 writing revision task. *Studies in Second Language Acquisition, 29*(1), 67–100.

Saito, H. (1994). Teachers' practices and students' preferences for feedback on second language writing: A case study of adult ESL learners. *TESL Canada Journal, 11*(2), 46–70.

Santa, T. (2006). *Dead letters: Error in composition, 1873–2004.* Cresskill, NJ: Hampton Press.

Santos, T. (1988). Professors' reactions to the academic writing of nonnative–speaking students. *TESOL Quarterly, 22,* 69–90.

Sarton, M. (1974). The rewards of living a solitary life. Retrieved from http:// karrvakarela. blogspot. com/2005/07/rewards-of-living-solitary-life. html

Scarcella, R.C. (1996). Secondary education in California and second language research. *CATESOL Journal, 9*(1), 129–152.

Scarcella, R.C. (2003). *Accelerating academic English: A focus on the English learner.* Berkeley: University of California Press.

Schiffren, L. (1996). Gay marriage, an oxymoron. *The New York Times,* March 23, 1996.

Schmidt, R. (1994). Deconstructing consciousness in search of useful definitions for applied linguistics. *AILA Review, 11,* 11–26.

Schmitt, N. (2010): *Research vocabulary: A vocabulary research manual.* Hampshire, U.K.: Palgrave Macmillan.

Schmitt, N., & Schmitt, D. (2005). *Focus on vocabulary.* New York: Longman.

Schuemann, C. (2008). Myth 2: Teaching citation is someone else's job. In J. Reid (Ed.), *Writing myths: Applying second language research to classroom teaching* (pp. 18–41). Ann Arbor: University of Michigan Press.

Semke, H. (1984). The effects of the red pen. *Foreign Language Annals, 17,* 195–202.

Seymour, S., & Walsh, L. (2006). *Essentials of teaching academic reading.* Boston: Houghton Mifflin.

Shaughnessy, M.P. (1977). *Errors and expectations.* New York: Oxford University Press.

Sheen, Y. (2007). The effect of focused written corrective feedback and language aptitude on ESL learners' acquisition of articles. *TESOL Quarterly, 41,* 255–283.

Sheppard, K. (1992). Two feedback types: Do they make a difference? *RELC Journal, 23,* 103–110.

Silva, T. (1988). Comments on Vivian Zamel's "Recent research on writing pedagogy." *TESOL Quarterly, 22,* 517–519.

Silva, T. (1990). Second language composition instruction: Developments, issues, and directions in ESL. In B. Kroll (Ed.), *Second language writing: Research insights for the classroom* (pp. 11–23). Cambridge, U.K.: Cambridge University Press.

Silva, T. (1993). Toward an understanding of the distinct nature of L2 writing: The ESL research and its implications. *TESOL Quarterly, 27,* 657–677.

Sommers, N. (1980). Revision strategies of student writers and experienced adult writers. *College Composition and Communication, 31,* 378–388.

Sommers, N. (1982). Responding to student writing. *College Composition and Communication, 33,* 148–156.

Spack, R. (1988). Initiating ESL students into the academic discourse community: How far should we go? *TESOL Quarterly, 22,* 29–51.

Spack, R. (2006). *Guidelines: A cross-cultural reading/writing text* (3rd Ed.). Cambridge, U.K.: Cambridge University Press.

Straub, R. (1997). Students' reactions to teacher comments: An exploratory study. *Research in the Teaching of English, 31,* 91–119.

Swales, J. (1990). *Genre analysis: English in academic and research settings.* Cambridge, U.K.: Cambridge University Press.

Swan, M., & Smith, B. (2001). *Learner English: A teacher's guide to interference and other problems.* Cambridge, U.K.: Cambridge University Press.

Tardy, C.M. (2009). *Building genre knowledge.* West Lafayette, IN: Parlor Press.

Truscott, J. (1996). The case against grammar correction in L2 writing classes. *Language Learning, 46,* 327–369.

Truscott, J. (1999). The case for "the case for grammar correction in L2 writing classes": A response to Ferris. *Journal of Second Language Writing, 8,* 111–122.

Truscott, J. (2004). Evidence and conjecture: A response to Chandler. *Journal of Second Language Writing, 13,* 337–343.

Truscott, J. (2007). The effect of error correction on learners' ability to write accurately. *Journal of Second Language Writing, 16,* 255–272.

Truscott, J. (2009). Arguments and appearances: A response to Chandler. *Journal of Second Language Writing, 18,* 59–60.

Truscott, J., & Hsu, A. Y-P. (2008). Error correction, revision, and learning. *Journal of Second Language Writing, 17,* 292–305.

Valdés, G. (1992). Bilingual minorities and language issues in writing: Toward professionwide responses to a new challenge. *Written Communication, 9* (1), 85–136.

van Beuningan, C., de Jong, N.M., & Kuiker, F. (in press). Evidence on the effectiveness of comprehensive error correction in Dutch multilingual classrooms. *Language Learning.*

Vann, R., Lorenz, F., & Meyer, D. (1991). Error gravity: Faculty response to errors in written discourse of nonnative speakers of English. In L. Hamp-Lyons (Ed.), *Assessing second language writing in academic contexts* (pp. 181–195). Norwood, NJ: Ablex.

Vann, R., Meyer, D., & Lorenz, F. (1984). Error gravity: A study of faculty opinion of ESL errors. *TESOL Quarterly, 18,* 427–440.

Wall, S., & Hull, G. (1989). The semantics of error: What do teachers know? In C.M. Anson (Ed.), *Writing and response: Theory, practice, and research* (pp. 261–292). Urbana, IL: NCTE.

Wardhaugh, R. (1970). The contrastive analysis hypothesis. *TESOL Quarterly, 4,* 123–130.

Warschauer, M., & Ware, P. (2006). Automated writing evaluation: Defining the classroom research agenda. *Language Teaching Research, 10,* 157–180.

Williams, J.M. (1981). The phenomenology of error. *College Composition and Communication, 32,* 152–168.

Wydick, R.C. (2005). *Plain English for lawyers* (5th Ed.). Durham: Carolina Academic Press.

Xue, G., & Nation, I.S.P. (1984). A university word list. *Language Learning and Communication, 3,* 215–229.

Zamel, V. (1982). Writing: The process of discovering meaning. *TESOL Quarterly, 16*(2), 195–209.

Zamel, V. (1985). Responding to student writing. *TESOL Quarterly, 19,* 79–102.

Zhang, S. (1995). Reexamining the affective advantage of peer feedback in the ESL writing class. *Journal of Second Language Writing, 4,* 209–222.

Zwier, L.J., & Bennett, G.R. (2006). *Teaching a lexis-based academic writing course.* Ann Arbor: University of Michigan Press.

Index